UNDERSTANDING
APOCALYPTIC LITERATURE

A Guide to the Book of Revelation

Mark Roberts

Cover design by Brian Harber.
Interior layout by Rachel Greene for elfinpen designs

Lower Lights Publications - Bedford, Texas
MarkRobertsBooks.com

Printed in the United States of America

ISBN 10: 1-890119-26-1
ISBN 13: 978-1-890119-26-3

To my wife Dena

You are my beloved and you are my friend.
I am my beloved's and my beloved is mine.

SONG OF SOLOMON 5:16B; 6:3

To my wife Dena

You are my beloved and you are my friend.
I am my beloved's and my beloved is mine.

SONG OF SOLOMON 5:16B; 6:3

Contents

Foreword

Understanding Apocalyptic Literature is a valuable contribution to the study of the last book of the New Testament. The original sources from which Mark Roberts gleans his information do not sit on most of our book shelves. Apocalyptic literature, aside from parts of Ezekiel, Daniel, and Zechariah, is unfamiliar territory, and some of us never venture into a study of it. Understandably, some Christians do not even have a ready knowledge of the biblical books mentioned above. Yet the patterns of apocalyptic thought, which were more familiar to the Christians of John's time than they are to us today, provide helpful insights into what John communicated in the book we call Revelation.

Perhaps if our English translations would have used *Apocalypse* rather than Revelation as the title of John's book, they might have opened for us a door of opportunity. This door would lead into a room filled with books somewhat similar in style to Revelation. But we are so far removed in time from the world of apocalyptic literature that we still might not have grasped the significance of the title *Apocalypse*. Apocalyptic works were filled with incidents of persons who were transported into a heavenly, otherworldly realm. They experienced visions about God, Jesus, the Devil, and both good and bad angels. They saw these visions during a time in which saints were suffering persecution on this earth. And they transcribed what they saw by means of highly figurative language that involved repetitious numbers and described weird creatures, cosmic upheavals, and bloody wars. Thus, understandably, we have difficulty making sense of the mysterious scenes they recorded.

Thankfully, in steps Mark Roberts, who helps us to understand Revelation. He accomplishes his task by exploring with us how authors of apocalyptic literature often used a variety of common techniques. He shows us that the main theme of Revelation is quite simple: "God is sovereign so be faithful." When persecution causes suffering, just hang in there. Jesus is victorious, and the saints will triumph in Him. Obviously, numerous minor themes are woven into the tapestry of John's book, but they serve its main purpose.

Understanding Apocalyptic Literature is as practical as it is insightful. Mark displays a remarkable talent in presenting a scholarly analysis of apocalyptic themes that is reverent, straightforward, and readable. He writes with the training of a specialist, but communicates in a way that all of us can understand.

Brother Roberts attended Florida College (1982–83) and went on to receive degrees from the University of Texas at Tyler (1985) and Abilene Christian University (1998). Previously published works include *The Five Daily Bible Reading Schedule*, with a *Reading Companion* to accompany it; *Seeking God's Way*, and *Who Will Follow Jesus?* He began preaching in 1985 and currently works with the Westside church of Christ in Irving, Texas. His wife Dena and two daughters Rebecca and Sara attest to his devotion as both husband and father. I have had the privilege of knowing Mark for nearly 25 years, and I am honored to be his close friend and brother in Christ.

Revelation is such an important book, and *Understanding Apocalyptic Literature* will help you immensely in your personal study. I would not minimize the importance of reading commentaries that delve verse by verse into the text of Revelation and elaborate in great detail such matters as authorship, date, and destination. If one is not careful, however, he or she can become discouraged by the immensity of material. But *Understanding Apocalyptic Literature* is fresh and concise; it is a much needed guide. I heartily recommend that you read it.

Melvin D. Curry, Ph.D.
Former Chair of Biblical Studies
Florida College

Acknowledgments

Books do not occur in a vacuum. Authors like to pretend that they could squirrel themselves away from everyone else and magically produce, on their own, their books. But of course, we carry with us at all times the people who influence, guide, and help us. Thus even if I were to find some deserted spot to write, I would still be a debtor to all who have assisted me and shaped me.

With this book those influences and helpers were easy to identify...

Dr. Wendell Willis taught a class on apocalyptic literature that I took in 1995 as I worked on a Master's Degree at ACU. That class became the seed for all that is here because it helped me realize how little I knew about apocalyptic literature. By the end of the class I was positively determined to fix that deficiency. Dr. Mitchell Reddish's book *Apocalyptic Literature: A Reader* was used in that class. It pulled together many different apocalyptic texts all in one place so that the students could begin to see what apocalyptic is about. I recommend Dr. Reddish's book enthusiastically, read from it regularly, and could not have written my book without it.

The folks who tirelessly proofread the manuscript are people I cannot thank enough. Erin Sullivan, Melvin Curry, Randy Mashburn, Warren and Paula Berkley, my sister Julie Clevenger, and my wife Dena used up gallons of red ink to make this book better for every reader. Melvin Curry's contributions far exceeded just proofreading. He proved to be a vital encouragement to me in this project.

Warren Berkley is all that anyone could ever ask for in a friend and co-worker in God's kingdom and then some. He constantly opens doors of opportunity for me and then pushes me through them.

The Westside church, and particularly her elders, compose a spiritual family of love, faithfulness and vibrancy that many Christians can only dream of. This church drives me to study harder, think clearer, preach better, and to always, *always* make truth practical while caring for and supporting me and my family in an incredible way. No preacher could ever want for more.

And finally, my family has always been a tremendous source of strength for me. My parents make up an unapologetic fan club of all I do. My sister and brother-in-law and their children, Truth and Patience, fill life with joy and happiness. My own daughters, Becca and Sara, applauded enthusiastically, feigned interest in obscure works like 4 Ezra amazingly well, and continually believed in their dad. Their mother, and my wife of 27 years, stands behind me with unqualified love and support for all my dreams, goals, and work in God's kingdom.

I
Why This Book?

Imagine a man, perhaps a neighbor or friend, heading out to his mailbox to get the mail. He finds the usual assortment of bills, catalogs, and magazines. Suddenly, an envelope attracts his attention. It is a big envelope with a picture of a celebrity shouting out that he is a finalist to win a giant cash prize. Incredibly, almost unbelievably, this phenomenal sweepstakes offer has arrived to announce he may have already won *twenty-five million dollars*!

Would anyone be excited for him? Should he be excited? $25 million would put most people into a better income bracket. Life would be significantly changed (hopefully for the better) by such a prize. What should this fellow do? Should he immediately fill out the entrance certificate, order lots of magazines and then begin planning how to protect such a large prize from the greedy hands of the IRS and his lazy relatives?

Probably not. For most people, such envelopes arrive so routinely that they are filed without much thought in the kitchen garbage along with yesterday's coffee grounds. If someone proudly announced, "I'm a finalist to win millions of dollars," many would have a hard time keeping a straight face while others would simply say "You and every other mailbox-owning American." We know, as do most people, that the sweepstakes offers that reach us by mail are come-ons to sell magazines. People understand what these sweepstakes offers are really about and so do not take them seriously.

What do sweepstakes mailings have to do with understanding the book of Revelation? This kind of mail helps us with Revelation, a letter mailed to seven churches in the first century, by showing how practical knowing *genre* is. "Genre?" one asks. "What is genre?" Genre is a term that means "a kind or sort" or "a category of artistic, musical, or literary composition characterized by a particular style, form, or content."[1] While it may not be a word that regularly comes up in typical conversation, all us of know and use the idea of genre every day.

Because we are so familiar with the *genre* of sweepstakes solicitations, we immediately toss them into the trash. We recognize "the kind or sort" as "junk mail" and we pitch it out. We have learned we will not win. We understand how this genre of mail works. Indeed that recognition is so important that the junk mail companies often actively try to fake genre, marking the envelope "Official Business Only" or with other

indicators that this envelope is very important and certainly not a worthless sweepstakes offer. Yet even if we are fooled into opening the envelope, as soon as we see all the magazine ads, we recognize the genre, and throw it away.

Sweepstakes offers fit so perfectly into the genre of junk mail that we usually do not even have to open them to know what they are and what they contain. Junk mail is a category of mail, "marked by a distinctive style, form or content." The big printing, the colorful envelope, the computer printed address that misspells the street name—it all clues the recipient immediately to what is inside. Out it goes, unopened. Would such ever happen with an envelope from the electric company?

Of course not. The mail from the electric company fits another genre (known as "bills") and again, without even opening the envelope, we know what is inside because we recognize "the kind or sort" of mail that it is.

Bible students who want to understand the book of Revelation need to know it has its own genre. The genre of Revelation is a powerful and unique type or class that signaled first century readers to the content of Revelation's message. They knew from the opening lines of John's writing what the book of Revelation would say to them and how it would say it. How could they know? For them it was simple. They knew the genre. This means if we want to read Revelation as its New Testament audience did, we as well must know that book's genre. What were their expectations of an apocalypse? What did they believe was in that "envelope" from Patmos?

Answering these questions is the foundation for understanding Revelation.

Unfortunately, not much is said or done with the genre of Revelation. Bible students have long recognized there are different genres in the material that makes up the Scriptures. For example, Proverbs has its own style. It is not Romans or Hebrews. It is not meant to be read or used as we would a New Testament epistle. If we try to force it into that mold, we will twist and wreck its meaning. Likewise, Psalms is not Matthew. In the Psalms we find its authors using powerful metaphors, similes and figures of speech all in poetic forms. Matthew is a Gospel, with an entirely different style and emphasis. No one would treat Psalms like Matthew, for such would destroy the message the human author, and ultimately God as the Author behind that author, intended to convey.

Thus, much work has been done throughout the Bible to research and understand the different genres the Holy Spirit used in inspiring the sacred Scriptures. Coming to terms with different genres in the Bible can be one of the most rewarding and fascinating studies any Bible student ever does. Yet the genre of Revelation seems to have eluded this kind of study. It is not doctrine, or strictly an epistle, or gospel, or even chronicled history. Revelation, and a few other books in the Bible like Daniel and Ezekiel, are part of the genre known as apocalyptic. This kind of writing was common in Bible times. We even have many examples of non-inspired apocalyptic writing to school us in the use of this genre, how it works, what it means, and how to understand it. Unfortunately, it is a genre that is still very unfamiliar to readers today. An examination of the apocalyptic genre, especially by using the apocalyptic material written in the Intertestamental Period (between the close of Malachi and beginning of Matthew) will help us to understand how apocalyptic works and what the original readers expected of books like the book of Revelation.

A good starting point for understanding this genre might be to get a good definition of the word "apocalyptic." *Apocalyptic* is a word that has come to be associated with doom and destruction, usually at the world's end. Indeed, "apocalypse" has become nearly a synonym today for "Armageddon" and the end of the world. In nearly any spy-thriller movie there is sure to be a stolen nuclear weapon and a dramatic moment in which the hero says (very dramatically, of course), "If that thing goes off, it will destroy the city in a fiery apocalypse!" That may be true, but we would do well to ask our superhero to hand back the word "apocalypse" and quit mangling its usage before he disarms the latest threat to human civilization. The term apocalypse does not always mean doom and despair.

Biblically, an apocalypse is a book that uses visions and dramatic word pictures to convey information about God's activity, particularly regarding the oppression of God's people by their enemies. Books that have this kind of common theme are called apocalypses or are said to be "apocalyptic."

It is important to know that this kind of material was not rare or uncommon in New Testament times. There were many of these kinds of books. With names like *2 Baruch*, *2 Enoch*, the *Apocalypse of Abraham*, the *War Scroll*, and *4 Ezra* they appear mysterious and strange to us. Yet, if one reads them, quickly one will be amazed to find passages that sound like they came straight from John's pen and the book of Revelation.

This kind of study does pose some difficulties. We will find it does not mesh with the contemporary trend of demanding Revelation be about our times and interpreting everything to fit that desire. Many would rather pay attention to the "signs" of the times and breathlessly talk about the latest seer who has found the book of Revelation to be speaking of 9/11's tragedies, the nation of Israel, global warming, terrorism and impending nuclear war (often termed, for dramatic effect, "nuclear Armageddon," something apparently more terrifying than generic Armageddon). However, ignoring genre can have severe ramifications.

What of those who do not understand the Nigerian emails that promise the sender will share part of $67 million found in a long lost bank account? That genre is known as a "scam" or "hoax," and people who do not realize it can end up losing large sums of money. Likewise, when people come to Revelation without taking any thought of the genre, usually nothing but problems follow. Again and again, whole theologies of the end times have been cranked out of Revelation that are clearly fantastic and ridiculous. For example, in the early second century a female prophet (whose name is unknown) was so excited about pinpointing the exact location of where the New

Jerusalem would descend that she claimed she saw a vision of Jesus dressed as a woman![2] The Crusades, a disaster all the way around by most accounts, were fueled by date setting that came directly out of Revelation. Since the end of the world was at hand (and that was a thousand years ago!), the best way to make ready the way of the Lord was clearing Jerusalem of the infidels.[3] Thousands (on both sides) died as a result of a misunderstanding of apocalyptic literature. Incredibly, even Christopher Columbus may have been acting out a scenario of the end time, which he derived from considering the millennial prophecies of Scripture.[4]

We chuckle at such naïvetè but acting irrationally as a result of misunderstanding biblical apocalyptic continues even in our times. In 1983 David Koresh, the leader of a cult based outside of Waco, Texas, ended up at odds with the authorities over a variety of very serious legal charges, as he and his followers stockpiled weapons and ammunition at his "Mount Carmel" compound. When law enforcement authorities tried to storm the compound, four ATF agents were killed in the raid. That led to an FBI siege of "Mount Carmel" with negotiators trying to talk Koresh and his disciples into a peaceful surrender. Talks stalled out as Koresh rambled almost endlessly about his particular slant on Revelation's meaning and how he was opening its seals. The FBI lacked any understanding of how Revelation worked or what it meant, which did not help much. It all ended horribly when Koresh set fire to his compound, burning it to the ground with him and his followers (and their children) still in it. The end result of Koresh's fanciful views of himself and the book of Revelation was that he and nearly all of his disciples died. Sadly, if the world stands long enough, Koresh probably will not be the last one to bring a catastrophe upon himself, his disciples, and innocent bystanders. Over and over apocalyptic material is tortured and twisted to fit what present day date-setters and news watchers want it to mean. They do not understand Revelation's genre; consequently, they cannot understand Revelation.

This kind of radical approach may drive an equally disappointing overreaction in the other direction by some Bible students. They decide Revelation must be the abode of extremists and nuts. Thus, many think that the way to handle Revelation is to read the first three chapters (the stuff to the seven churches) and then to get out of the book before the weird parts start up. As a result, the powerful message of the New Testament's apocalyptic book is lost.

Yet, it really does not take too much to get a handle on apocalyptic literature. Apocalypse is a word that means a "revelation, disclosure" or "disclosing secrets belonging to the last days."[5] While realizing apocalyptic literature is more than just an ordinary revelation of God's will, it can be understood if we understand how this genre works. The very purpose of this genre is to disclose and reveal! If we can gain even an elementary appreciation for the style of writing, if we can get in the author's mind and understand why someone would write an apocalypse, and if we can compare what we have in Scripture to the common apocalypses that circulated in New Testament times, we can make right use of the Bible's apocalyptic literature because we will be using apocalyptic as it was intended to be used. That is the goal of this book.

Our course is mapped out: we will examine the genre "apocalyptic" to learn what it is about and how to use and understand it rightly. As we do this, we will read from non-inspired apocalyptic and inspired apocalyptic both so that we can better understand Revelation's message and style. Be warned: if one is carrying around a large load of preconceptions about Revelation or the end times or the return of the Lord, this study may make mincemeat out of all such notions. As noted above, so much of what is gleaned out of Revelation is just mistaken or even dead wrong. Be prepared to see Revelation and other apocalyptic material in a new way. These ideas may make some people very unhappy, but for those who are genuinely trying to understand what God has to say, this exploration of how God is presenting His Word through the special and exciting genre of apocalyptic will be tremendously rewarding.

II

What Makes Apocalyptic Literature Apocalyptic?

The year 1861 was a time of crisis for the United States of America. Abolitionists were fighting against slavery, and soon, the entire country would be plunged into a horrible caldron of war and bloodshed. In the midst of it all, Julia Ward Howe, an abolitionist, decided the popular tune "John Brown's Body" needed words more fitting and rousing. So she wrote:

"Mine eyes have seen the glory of the coming of the Lord; He is trampling out the vintage where the grapes of wrath are stored. He hath loosed the fateful lightning of His terrible swift sword; His truth is marching on."

Frederic J. Baumgartner, in his wonderful survey of history through the eyes of groups that believed the end of the world was imminent, notes "it is difficult to imagine that the whole of apocalyptic thought could be summed up better and in fewer words."[6]

Interestingly, many sing the *Battle Hymn of the Republic* today with little thought to its apocalyptic overtones. Could this be because most people are not sure what makes something apocalyptic?

What earns a book the classification "apocalyptic"? What kind of material fits into that category or class? We easily understand what makes a sweepstakes offer junk mail. What does a book need to have in it to be considered apocalyptic?

Fortunately, a great deal of work has been done to define what is (and is not) apocalyptic. While "laymen" sometimes shy away from Bible scholars and their lofty discussions (and sometimes for good reason), the Society for Biblical Literature's apocalyptic project provides an excellent starting point for a consideration of apocalyptic literature. After much work and debate, considering and reading a wide of variety of apocalyptic materials, they defined apocalyptic as "A genre of revelatory literature with a narrative framework, in which a revelation is mediated by an otherworldly being to a human recipient, disclosing a transcendent reality which is both temporal, insofar as it envisages eschatological salvation and spatial insofar as it involves another, supernatural world."[7] Later, they added, "intended to interpret present earthly circumstances in light of the supernatural world of the future, and to influence both the understanding and the behavior of the audience by means of divine authority."[8]

That definition may be a bit academic in its tone, but its key points are not that difficult. First, this definition says an apocalyptic work is *revelatory literature*. This means it claims to come from God. Not everything written to godly people about spiritual themes and ideas makes that claim. For example, there is plenty of (non-inspired) wisdom literature that plainly says it is the collected observations and wisdom of men, not God. The wise sage is not saying, "God told me this" or "Thus saith the Lord." He says "This is what I saw" or "Here is what I concluded is wise." Apocalyptic literature, however, very clearly announces and emphasizes this is the divine word coming directly from heaven.

Secondly, it contains a *narrative framework*. In other words, it tells a story. Again, not all spiritual writings do that. The Gospel of Thomas (a non-inspired gospel account) contains no stories about Jesus. It consists of numerous lines of "and Jesus said" followed by a saying purported to be Jesus' and then another "and Jesus said" followed by another saying. There is no narration of Jesus' life, and no telling of what Jesus did. Epistles also lack a narrative framework. They are straightforward exhortation, telling the reader what to believe and do. Apocalyptic contains exhortation, but the exhortations are woven into a story line. Apocalyptic has a plot. It says, "An angel came and told me that a horrible fire-breathing beast would arise to slaughter the people of righteousness, but then another mighty angel would come from the East with a fiery sword in his hand..." This well illustrates how easy it is to be drawn into apocalyptic literature because it relates a story. One of the reasons that Revelation is so interesting to so many is that it is the very antithesis of dry, doctrinal discourse. Crazy stuff happens in Revelation! That stuff makes up a story, an important part of apocalyptic literature.

Notice the beginning point: "an angel told me." *Otherworldly beings* are a big part of what defines apocalyptic literature. How does this divine account, this story of what is happening and will happen, get into the author's hands? An angel or some other divine being arrives and says, "Write this down" or "Watch this and tell others." Angels play a leading role in apocalyptic literature because they give the material significant authority. No one wants to read a book that begins like this: "Well, here is my opinion about what we ought to do in this crisis, but, of course, I am just a fallible human so who knows if I am right or wrong?" Apocalyptic literature comes on strong, with power and authority: "A mighty angel showed me how these terribly dark days will finally end."

Third, the Society of Biblical Literature (SBL) definition says apocalyptic literature *discloses a reality on two levels, temporal and spatial.* This is, in this writer's estimation, the single most important characteristic of apocalyptic literature. Apocalyptic literature radically shifts our view of world events because it proposes that what we see here on this earth is just the playing out of a much larger reality: what is happening in heaven. An apocalypse says, "See that persecution going on over there? That is happening because Satan and his forces attacked God!" It says, "The fall of that world empire came about because God willed it, not because the empire was weak militarily."

Apocalyptic literature lets us look "behind the curtain" to see the real origins of what happens around us. People on earth may think they are doing so much and are so important, but an apocalyptic work would reveal they are just pawns and that there are greater spiritual forces at work in a much bigger battle than many realize. In fact, apocalyptic says that no one can understand the world by looking at current events because such a view fails to account for the actions of God and His angels, and of course, the devil and his minions. According to apocalyptic, this world is not isolated from the heavenly world. In many ways, this view is the very opposite of deism. Apocalyptic proposes a dual view of reality, arguing that what is happening in the heavenly realm is reflected in the earthly events seen around us.

In the song "Glory, Glory, Hallelujah" we see the very earthy event of the coming war depicted in this way. The Civil War is not a political struggle that finally overflowed onto battlefields between two opposing armies. Julia Ward Howe would have none of that. The Civil War was the "coming of the Lord" as God unleashed the "grapes of wrath" and "loosed His terrible swift sword" so that truth could march on, and the evil of slavery would be completely judged and put down. That is an apocalyptic perspective on the Civil War, one full of the "two world" viewpoint that apocalyptic presses.

The last points of the definition are that apocalyptic proposes *eschatological salvation* and *to influence behavior*. Being concerned with eschatological salvation means that apocalyptic reveals that at the end (eschatology refers to the doctrine of the end times) God will move decisively to save His people. The crisis is raging, the Lord's people are powerless, the situation has never looked blacker, and then suddenly, God will act, and His people will be saved. All of this writing was done, of course, not just as an academic exercise, but to change what people do. Apocalyptic writing conveys the message, "Hang on just a bit longer, do not give up, do not join up with paganism or the forces attacking the righteous. Keep serving God!" Revelation brims with this kind of material (for example, Revelation 2:10). In every way possible, the apocalyptic writer tries to convince his audience that redemption is coming soon, so defecting over to evil is foolish. The righteous will be exalted and glorified in the day of the new world while all evildoers will be tortured and burnt and killed and generally rue the day they were ever born. Thus, believing apocalyptic literature influences the reader, and it decidedly alters our behavior.

Perhaps the SBL definition can be crystallized into something that is not quite such a large mouthful or so difficult to explain. Here is a working definition of apocalyptic literature: "a story, written in a time of crisis and distress, that is given by otherworldly beings explaining how God will reverse everything so the righteous will triumph." That is apocalyptic in a nutshell.

Before moving forward with that definition to better understand how apocalyptic literature accomplishes its goals, it is important to consider the writers of apocalyptic. We need to look at the mindset of an author who would write one of these "stories, in a time of crisis, received from otherworldly beings, which explains how God will triumph." In the next chapter, therefore, we examine who writes apocalyptic and why. We will find that getting inside the author's mind is tremendously helpful in understanding what apocalyptic wants to do.

III
Why Apocalyptic?

Why does an author write an apocalypse? What motivates someone to graphically describe God's final triumph in the end of all things as a bloody battle over a terrible beast? Any attempt to understand apocalyptic literature begins with comprehending the apocalyptic mind set. We must acknowledge that no single motivation can account for all apocalyptic material, and also understand that some times we may not know all we want about a specific document's background. That being said, it is possible for us to understand much of the apocalyptic mindset and thus to understand apocalyptic literature itself.

A great deal of the available uninspired apocalyptic literature comes from the time between the Old and New Testaments, often referred to as the Intertestamental Period. The four hundred years between Malachi and Matthew serve very well to illustrate the kind of events that give rise to apocalyptic thought and thus to apocalyptic writing.

As the Jewish people stepped into these centuries, the book that perhaps buoyed them more than any other was Daniel. Its incredible visions and terrifying figures, all weaving together a tapestry that depicted the eventual triumph of God's people, made it unlike anything else in Scripture. For certain, Isaiah, Zechariah and Ezekiel all contain visions that remind the reader of Revelation in style and even content. But it is Daniel that brings together all the pieces to offer a reassuring and comforting message unlike any other book in the Old Testament. It is no surprise, therefore, that during the Intertestamental Period, when things went badly for the Jews and as they longed to hear a message from God, that books like Daniel were born. A writer took pen in hand and announced, "If God were to talk to us, this is what He would say... ." The non-inspired books adopted the apocalyptic form, which had been used by Daniel, in order to convey to their contemporaries a sense of urgency, a need for faithfulness, and an outlook of certainty that would sustain them during their own crisis. They set a standard for the kind of writing that God's people would look to in hard times—the kind of times the readers of Revelation would experience in the first century.

This provides a fine place to note apocalyptic literature's debt to the Old Testament. Apocalyptic literature shares close ties to the Bible's prophetic books and its wisdom books. This is true for inspired apocalyptic material, like Daniel, and in some ways, even more, for the uninspired material written between the Testaments. The prophetic voice of God's certain judgment rings out against all who would profane His name and Temple. Wisdom literature's admonitions about the wise way to do and live dominate the admonitions of apocalyptic. Throughout all apocalyptic literature, the Old Testament is continually alluded to and referenced. Evil kingdoms are called "Sodom and Gomorrah" or "Egypt." Noah, Enoch, Abraham and other Old Testament heroes appear prominently in many apocalyptic writings. This means that while understanding genre (the purpose of this book) is crucially important, genre alone cannot unlock apocalyptic literature's meaning. To fully appreciate and understand apocalyptic there must be some understanding of the history and the characters of the Old Testament and of God's law and expectations for His people. Apocalyptic can only be understood against the backdrop of the Old Testament. In the Old Testament, its events and story, particularly Israel's continued sin of idolatry and subsequent punishment, give rise to a new way of expressing God's warning and comfort to His people. That is the inspired, authoritative apocalyptic of Isaiah, Daniel, Ezekiel and Joel. By the time of the Intertestamental Period that dramatic and powerful way of speaking was being adapted and shaped further by uninspired writers into the form that the New Testament readers of Revelation would be familiar with and know. But it all still rests on and sprang from the seeds of the Old Testament.

Let us now explore a little further the events of the Intertestamental Period that caused writers to put pen to paper and construct apocalyptic material for their times. What was happening in the Intertestamental Period that drove apocalyptic writing among the Jews in Palestine? The answer is trouble and persecution of every kind. For orthodox Jewish peoples, the Intertestamental Period was a very difficult time. Alexander the Great had conquered the world. He was committed to bringing Greek culture, Greek thought, and Greek ways of doing things to every corner of the empire, including Judea. To a great extent his quest to Hellenize the world was successful. However, in Judea a culture war was fought. Some thought "going Greek" was fine and that everyone should "get with it." Others were just as certain that God's people must not "get with it." Their concern was that their distinctive Jewish identity, language, and law would all be lost in the oncoming tide of all things Greek. The concerns of those who protested the invasion of Hellenism seemed to be validated when the various kings and tyrants who ruled after Alexander tried ferociously to stamp out the Jewish religion and replace it with Greek idolatry.

One of the most famous Jewish warriors of all time, Judas Maccabee, emerged during this crisis. Under his leadership the culture war went hot, becoming a literal war. Judas was the son of a priest, Mattathias. When Mattathias was ordered to sacrifice to a pagan god, he refused and attacked the soldiers who were trying to force such a sacrifice. The old priest then led his family to the hills of Judea where they waged a surprisingly successful guerilla war against the Syrians who had occupied Judea. After he died, one of his sons, Judas, took over the leadership of the revolt. Antiochus Epiphanes, the Syrian king ruling over Judea, had desecrated the temple in Jerusalem in December 167 BC by offering pig flesh upon the altar and daring to enter into the Most Holy Place. Incredibly, Judas and his armies regained control of Jerusalem in 165 BC and purified the Temple. In the annals of military history, the success of Judas' relatively small armies against much larger foes remains as one of the classic examples of how highly motivated people can overcome almost anything to throw invaders out of their homeland.

Some of this history was glorious, and the Jews reveled in their independence. Yet, there were still hard questions to ask and to answer. How could God have let a Syrian desecrate His temple? Further, despite being somewhat free for a few years under the Maccabees, the Jews still knew their standing in the world. They were a pitifully tiny country under constant threat to be subjugated by just about any second-rate power that wanted to oppress them. God did not seem to defend or fight for Judah anymore. Again, this had become apparent when Antiochus marched into the Holy of Holies, and was *not* struck down for his transgression. While the Maccabees did get a guerilla force organized, the Jews had no delusions of being able to re-establish the empire of David in all its splendor and size. What had gone wrong?

To top matters off, the Jews of the Intertestamental Period were keenly aware that they had lost the prophetic voice of God. Several passages in the book of Maccabees state this very clearly: they "stored the stones (of the desecrated altar -MR) in a convenient place on the temple hill *until a prophet should come to tell what to do with them*" (1 Maccabees 4:46).[9] "So there was great distress in Israel, such as had not been since the time that prophets ceased to appear among them" (9:27).[10] God was no longer speaking directly to Israel, thus leaving Israel adrift (as they perceived it) in uncertainty. Where was the Golden Age the prophets had spoken of, with their promises of the re-establishment of the king, and the Davidic throne of Israel? These magnificent and longed for events did not seem to be happening, nor did they appear to be about to happen. What was going on?

The times were difficult and turbulent. When one combines the crisis of the times with a corresponding feeling of powerlessness and the loss of prophetic guidance, it is easy to see a mind-shift occurring among the Jews. It is this shift that begins to explain apocalyptic literature. With all the problems they were facing, the Jews began to feel as if there was one, and only one, solution to their overwhelming troubles: God. He would fix everything by decisively and suddenly intervening in judgment, establishing His messianic rule once and for all. Instead of the Jews bringing about good things by their faithfulness to God and His Law, increasingly they looked to God to do what they could not. Indeed, they realized that since they could not do it in their might, strength or military prowess, they must wait for God who would certainly accomplish what they could not. Hope began to migrate from this world and this age to another world and another age.[11] D.S. Russell's excellent introduction to Jewish apocalyptic notes, "Apocalyptic literature is essentially a literature of people who saw no hope for their nation in terms of politics or on the plain of history."[12] The Jews were saying, "We cannot do it. We cannot throw off the yoke of tyranny nor purify the corrupt leadership that rules over us, but God can and He will." That is the message of apocalyptic literature: God is about to do something dramatic for the faithful, and do it very soon. "Watch what will happen in our very lifetimes, all will be well, just you wait" is its main theme. Implicit in such thinking is the idea that one must remain faithful to God to enjoy the great blessings that were certainly soon to come when God powerfully and dramatically overturned all the evils of the hour and set all things right.

Thus, it is clear that one of the most important characteristics of the apocalyptic mind is a crisis. Not everyone may see the times as a crisis (some Jews embraced Hellenistic culture), but the writers of apocalyptic literature certainly saw that the sky was falling, very heavily, right now. Their pens moved in response to the terrors of the moment around them and to their inability to do anything about it. God will act. God will deliver. God will save. All one need do is wait, watch, and remain faithful.

This crisis mentality fits the book of Revelation very well. Revelation reveals that the churches to which it was written were under intense fire (see Revelation 2:3, 10, 13; 3:9). Yet, what could Christians do? They were part of an illegal religion. For many years Christianity had hid in the shadow of Judaism. This had been an effective strategy to keep the authorities at bay, but now Jews were working tooth and nail to expose Christianity as something entirely different from Judaism. Persecution descended upon the church. Christians had no military assets of any kind and no national standing. So again, in a crisis, apocalyptic literature provided much needed answers. What will happen to us? Does God care that we suffer? Will He act? Apocalyptic literature answered all of these questions and more. This makes apocalyptic a genre that speaks to its time. People of faith have always struggled with the questions of suffering. The crisis of their times forced apocalyptic writers to speak to those questions at the very highest or most intense level. At the beginning, or most elementary level of suffering, everyone asks, "Why is there pain and suffering in the world?" At an intermediate, second level, Christians then ask why good people suffer. Few people mind if a drug dealer is shot in a deal gone sour, but what if an innocent bystander is also gunned down? What if that bystander is a child? Why do good people know pain, particularly since evil people seem to be doing so well? Those difficult questions may, in a crisis, give way to an even higher level of questions. The question of the most profound importance is the question that comes from persecution: why do we suffer for being good? Why are we hurt precisely for being what God commands us to be? One writer noted, "[A]pocalyptic functioned as a kind of pictorial narrative theodicy which acknowledges the legitimacy of the inevitable question found not only on the lips of scoffers, namely, 'If there is a good God who is in control of things, why doesn't he do something about present evil?' The apocalyptists' response: 'He *will*, for history is a unified story which is not over yet.'"[13]

Apocalyptic is an answer to a crisis. It is material written to explain the unthinkable: persecution and suffering for being faithful to God. It is, in the main, an alternative doctrine to the idea of mankind's progress. The optimists and humanists among us believe that life will get better and better, and with technology and human goodness at work, this planet will be renovated and made perfectly wonderful if only enough time passes. Apocalyptic writers and believers uniformly say, "Are you kidding? Evil is at work, persecution is breaking out, the forces of darkness are subjugating the world, and nothing but God's mighty hand can straighten this mess out, and when He does—look out!" So apocalyptic remains forever a paradox: down on the present moment but promising a bright future to the faithful who can wait out the current crisis.

In conclusion, we have already learned much about how to read and understand apocalyptic literature. Whatever we make of the strange symbols and signs that Revelation (or other apocalyptic books in the Bible like Daniel) contains, it is clear that they must mean something to the people to whom those books were originally addressed. Those people were in a crisis, those people were suffering, and those books were written to help them understand the terrible times they were going through and live faithfully through them. In particular, fanciful notions that we can read today's headlines in Revelation are pushed back—simply because we better understand the motivation for writing apocalyptic literature.

Thomas G. Long noted in an article about preaching apocalyptic literature, "The apocalyptic literary genre does not happen by accident; it erupts under specific social and religious conditions. It is the voice the Christian faith necessarily speaks under certain circumstances, and that is why its loss must not be permitted."[14] Indeed, in a culture where persecution seems more possible than it has in years, the people of God may once again flock to the Bible's apocalyptic sections to be comforted by them as so many have before. Of course, by appreciating what it is to be harmed for being faithful, we gain more than comfort. We come to understand why someone would write an apocalypse and what that author desired that genre of literature to do for its audience. Thinking through the expectations apocalyptic literature's readers would have for this kind of material will be our task in the next chapter.

IV
What Would Revelation's Readers Expect?

One of the biggest breakthroughs for Bible students probing Revelation is realizing its material was not unique to its original readers. This may be a bit difficult because most people's experience with Revelation seems to confirm an opposite view: *nothing* else could possibly be like the book of Revelation. For example, on the walls of many Sunday school classrooms is the official picture of the "Bible library" portraying all the books of the Bible in their divisions. The five books of Law are together, as are the books of Poetry, and the Gospels and epistles. But in a grouping by itself, singularly alone, was that one book at the end of the Bible, Revelation. In most churches very little was ever said about that last book of the Bible, especially in children's classes. Daring to read the book, for many, just caused confusion and terror. It does not take long to conclude that Revelation is, without doubt, in a class by itself.

This would not have been the reaction of Revelation's original audience. In the first century apocalyptic material like Revelation circulated widely.[15] Larry Helyer writes in his book *Exploring Jewish Literature of the Second Temple Period* that such material "flourished in both Jewish and Christian circles during the last half of the first century AD."[16] Apocalyptic books were so prevalent that scholars now debate whether Revelation influenced their authors or if they perhaps influenced Revelation. George Nickelsburg, an internationally known specialist in the field of early Judaism and the origins of Christianity, notes that works like *1 Enoch* and *Jubilees* were considered authoritative in some circles, meaning they were certainly not obscure unknown works.[17] The ancient but highly respected commentary by Moses Stuart clues us into what we need to realize about apocalyptic literature in the first century: "To sum up all in a few words: John wrote in order to be read and understood; and therefore intelligent persons of his day might understand him. If they did, it was by virtue of familiarity with language and imagery such as he employed. Now whatever helps us to place ourselves in a situation like to that of John's original readers, helps us to read his book intelligently. It follows of course, that the apocryphal books, written at or near his time, which exhibit to us either the language or the style and imagery of that period, must afford us important aid in reading and understanding the Apocalypse."[18] Stuart correctly identifies the point this book wants to make: the original readers lived in a time when the genre of apocalyptic was common and they had access to all kinds of material that reads very much like Revelation. To understand Revelation as they did, to read it with their eyes, means we must understand apocalyptic literature as they did.

While there is not always complete agreement whether to classify a book as apocalyptic, scholars have identified at least fourteen works that are considered to be Jewish apocalyptic that were written before the first century AD.[19] Beyond these, there is the material in the Old Testament that is apocalyptic or contains major sections of apocalyptic material (Isaiah, Ezekiel, Daniel, and Zechariah). One should also add in the substantial amount of Christian apocalyptic and Jewish apocalyptic written in the first century. Beside all of this, there is a significant amount of material that, while not specifically classified as apocalyptic, is closely related to it and shares some of its themes and characteristics. All in all, this means in the first century AD there was no shortage of literature that read like the book of Revelation. One implication of this is that Revelation probably didn't have the "I have never read anything like this before!" impact on its first readers as it has now. Based on their experience with similar materials, they would have expectations of what Revelation would be and what it would do.

We must not forget that genre sets expectations. When one opens a party invitation he expects to find basic information such as the date and time for the party. It would be unusual and confusing if that information was not there. Party invites are *supposed* to tell the where and when of the party. Likewise, if someone says they have written a new classical symphony, no one expects them to whip out a kazoo and play a few bars of it. The genre of "classical music" does not normally include kazoo performances. Thus, just as people have strong expectations of what they will find when they open a sweepstakes offer or any other piece of junk mail, so Revelation's original recipients would have known what was "in the envelope" when Revelation was read in their assemblies. Grasping those expectations, what those first century readers thought and understood about apocalyptic, is essential to being able to understand Revelation properly. Revelation 1:1 begins the book by announcing it is "The revelation of Jesus Christ." The term "revelation" is the word "apocalypse." So what did the original readers of Revelation expect from a book that opens by claiming to be an apocalypse?

To begin with, those readers would expect that an apocalyptic book would take a two-world view of life. This is the concept of dualism discussed in chapter 2. Dualism means that what is happening here on this earth is not the whole story. There is much going on in the heavenly realm that is directly affecting life on earth because there are opposing forces battling for control of the universe. In short, good is fighting against evil. Apocalyptic literature attempts to pierce the veil and explain events *here* in light of what is happening *there*. This is a major feature of apocalyptic literature. This is seen, for example, in the book known as *4 Ezra*. Written late in the first century AD, *4 Ezra* provides a prime example of apocalyptic as written and understood in New Testament times. 4 Ezra 4:21 says, "For as the land is assigned to the forest and the sea to its waves, *so also those who dwell upon earth can understand only what is on the earth, and he who is above the heavens can understand what is above the height of the heavens.*" Without a revelation from God, without apocalyptic, people on earth will not understand what is happening. *2 Baruch* (also written late in the first century AD) illustrates this in chapters 7 and 8: "And after this I heard that angel saying to the angels that held the lamps, 'Destroy and throw down the wall to its foundations, So that the enemy cannot boast and say, We have torn down the wall of Zion, And we have burnt the place of the mighty God... then the angels did as he had commanded them." The destruction of Jerusalem that the writer is discussing is not, as his readers might have thought, the work of the Roman armies. No, "Baruch" says. It was done at the command of God by angels, not the Romans. The Dead Sea Scrolls contain the same idea in the *War Scroll*, where God is said to "raise up the kingdom of Michael in the midst of the gods and the realm of Israel in the midst of all flesh" (1 Qumran 17:6-8). Israel's rise to power is actually the rise of Michael and his armies and is the playing out of God's work in the heavenly realm!

The Bible's apocalyptic literature fits the dualism pattern perfectly. For example, in Daniel 10:13 we read why Daniel's prayers were not being answered. An angel tells him "The prince of the kingdom of Persia withstood me twenty-one days, but Michael, one of the chief princes, came to help me, for I was left there with the kings of Persia." The forces fighting against each other in the heavenly realm are hindering Daniel's prayers on earth. Revelation chapter 12 contains one of the clearest examples of dualism, an example considered to be a classic of this kind of thinking. John writes "Now war arose in heaven, Michael and his angels fighting against the dragon. And the dragon and his angels fought back, but he was defeated, and there was no longer any place for them in heaven. And the great dragon was thrown down, that ancient serpent, who is called the devil and Satan, the deceiver of the whole world—he was thrown down to the earth, and his angels were thrown down with him. And I heard a loud voice in heaven, saying, 'Now the salvation and the power and the kingdom of our God and the authority of his Christ have come, for the accuser of our brothers has been thrown down, who accuses them day and night before our God" (Revelation 12:7-10). Many, including this writer, believe this is a portrayal of the Calvary event. What is noteworthy is that Calvary is not talked about in terms of a cross and a hill outside Jerusalem; instead it is portrayed in terms of a war in heaven. From an earthly perspective, the text appears to describe what Jesus accomplished on the cross, but from John's apocalyptic, heavenly perspective, it was a spiritual victory in the battle between good and evil.

Naturally, if there is indeed another world hidden from ordinary man's view, someone will ask the apocalyptic writer,

"How did you come to manage this exclusive peek behind the scenes?"

This leads to the second expectation first century readers would have had for Revelation: otherworldly characters.

Angels and other creatures from beyond play a huge role in apocalyptic literature. Where do apocalyptic writers get their information about all God will soon do? An angel or other heavenly being comes and gives information and heavenly insights to the writer. Almost all apocalyptic literature features angelic beings who function as intermediaries, bridging the gap between earth and heaven. For example, in the *Apocalypse of Weeks* (written in the second century BC) the writer says, "I Enoch, according to that which appeared to me in the heavenly vision, and which I know from the words of the holy angels and understand from the tablets of heaven..." (1 Enoch 90:2). Although it is usually an angel that comes with this encouraging and comforting information, sometimes God Himself gives the scoop. In 4 Ezra 14:41-46 this is the claim made: "And my mouth was opened, and was no longer closed. *And the Most High gave understanding to the five men, and by turns they wrote what was dictated, in characters which they did not know.* They sat forty days... So during the forty days ninetyfour books were written. And when the forty days were ended, the Most High spoke to me, saying 'Make public the twentyfour books that you wrote first and let the worthy and the unworthy read them; but keep the seventy that were written last, in order to give them to the wise among your people."

Again, biblical apocalyptic literature fits this pattern exactly. Daniel receives visions and words from angels in Daniel 7:16ff; 8:16ff; 9:21ff; 10:5ff; 12:5ff. Ezekiel receives angelic information in 40:3-4 that guides the rest of the vision. Revelation stands as the example *par excellence*. In Revelation 1:11, John records that he is told, "Write what you see in a book and send it to the seven churches, to Ephesus and to Smyrna and to Pergamum and to Thyatira and to Sardis and to Philadelphia and to Laodicea." The One showing him these things is no less than Jesus the Christ. This auspicious beginning, however, does not prohibit other angels from showing up throughout the book to convey more information to John (see 5:2, 10:1, 17:7 and 19:9 for example).

First century readers would also expect Revelation to include a journey. In apocalyptic literature when one receives a revelation through an angel, he often takes a journey to heaven or otherworldly places. The writer of apocalyptic literature cannot always simply be told what will happen. Sometimes he must go and see so he will understand the mysteries that humans cannot fathom here on earth. The writer goes to heaven, gets wisdom and knowledge, and then comes back here to share it with those wise enough to understand. For example, in *1 Enoch* (from a section written in the third century BC) we find Enoch on his way to heaven: "And behold, I saw the clouds: and they were calling me in a vision, and the fogs were calling me; and the course of the stars and the lightnings were rushing me and... the winds were causing me to fly and rushing me high up into heaven" (1 Enoch 14:8). In the *Testament of Abraham* (written in the latter part of the first century AD) the same kind of heavenly trip occurs: "And the archangel Michael went down and took Abraham (and set him) on the cherubim chariot and lifted him up to the heights of heaven and acted as high guide on the cloud together with sixty angels... Take Abraham up to the first gate of heaven, so that he may view the judgements and the retributions there" (Testament of Abraham 10:1, 19). Both of these passages are highly reminiscent of Revelation 4:1: "After these things I looked, and *behold, a door standing open in heaven!* And the first voice which I heard was like a trumpet speaking with me, saying, *'Come up here,* and I will show you what must take place after this.'"

First century readers would expect as a matter of course in apocalyptic literature what befuddles and confuses readers today: signs and symbols of every sort. In this genre little is presented in straightforward fashion because it would not be inspiring or memorable. Apocalyptic literature wants to reveal its secrets in an unforgettable way. Of course, saying "apocalyptic wants to reveal its secrets" may surprise some. Many today teach that Revelation was written in code and thus must be decoded to be understood. Its message is hidden in code, we are told, so if it fell into enemy hands the enemy would not be able to understand it and persecute the church for its contents. This assertion is made so commonly that it is often accepted without anyone attempting to prove it. Yet, there is no evidence that anyone ever wrote a single apocalyptic document in any kind of deliberate code, or that the vision and symbols were ever intended to be a code. In fact, not all apocalyptic literature would have provoked persecution. If apocalyptic material did cause persecution, its authors would more than likely have welcomed it as proof of their faithfulness to God. Further, the apocalyptic "code" would not have been that hard to break. Does anyone really imagine Roman authorities could not figure out what the beast in Revelation symbolized? James Efird notes "The older idea that apocalyptic was written in a code so that the persecutors could not understand and thus further intimidate the persecuted people simply does not hold up under close examination. If the persecutors could read the symbolic vision, they could certainly read the explanation!"[20]

The truth is that apocalyptic visions were written not to keep secrets but to reveal them.[21] That is what the very term "apocalypse" means: to open, to reveal. In the *Animal Apocalypse* (written during the Maccabbean times, approximately 165 BC) the writer says, "And after this I saw another dream, and I will show the whole dream to you my son" (1 Enoch 85:1). John writes, "blessed is the one who reads aloud the words of this prophecy, and blessed are those who hear, and who keep what is written in it" (Revelation 1:3). Apocalyptic is, in many ways, like the gospel itself: foolishness to those who don't want to understand and life-giving and life-changing to any and all who will try to understand. It certainly does separate the enlightened from the fools who are perishing with this world. However, it is not encoded or impossible to understand. Apocalyptic is *trying* to help those who want to be faithful understand what God is doing in our world. The revelation from above is available to the "select few"—those who will heed the divine wisdom contained in the apocalyptic book.

So all those signs and weird happenings would not have intimidated Revelation's audience. They would have been well familiar with beasts terrorizing the faithful and stars falling from the heavens because that kind of imagery is a mainstay in apocalyptic literature.

The readers of Revelation would also have expected that this piece of apocalyptic literature would, like all other apocalyptic writings, propose a solution to the crisis at hand: God will crush evil and utterly triumph. As we have seen, apocalyptic is not written when all is well but instead tries to work out the problems and questions arising in hard times. Apocalyptic thus often features a confrontation of horrific evil and speaks of a giant action of God necessary to reform the world and rescue the godly.

That means apocalyptic will feature a cry for God's help. From *4 Ezra* we read, "How long and when will these things be? Why are our years few and evil?... Did not the souls of the righteous in their chambers ask about these matters, saying, 'How long are we to remain here? And when will come the harvest of our reward?'" (4 Ezra 4:33,35). In *2 Baruch* the cry is the same: "And I said, O Lord, my lord, have I come into the world for no other purpose than to see the evils of my mother?... But one thing I will ask of thee, O Lord. What is to happen to us? For if thou destroyest thy city and dost deliver up thy land to those that hate us, how will the name of Israel again be remembered?... Is the universe to return to its original state and the world to revert to primeval silence? Is the human race to be destroyed and mankind to be blotted out?" (2 Baruch 3:1-8). *2 Baruch* asks, "When will God act? What will the Lord do for us, and when?" Notice that both of these citations are early in their respective books. What would one expect the rest of *4 Ezra* and *2 Baruch* to discuss? Naturally, the destruction of the wicked for which the godly pine is a chief concern in these books. Do not fail to note the extent these "how long" sections are so very similar to Revelation 6:10's cry. This is a common mark of apocalyptic literature.

Often the answer to "how long?" necessitates a survey of human history, breaking it into periods or epochs so that the work of God in each time period can be easily identified. One of the reasons this is done is that by breaking history into periods, the readers can see how many periods remain till the end, and which period they are presently in. The other reason history is divided into periods is it gives the reader confidence that the Lord is controlling everything. It says that all history is under God's control.

Dividing history into time frames is almost a signature of apocalyptic. Daniel 9 divides remaining history into the famous seventy weeks. 1 Enoch 1-36 gives seventy "generations" from the Flood to the Final Judgment. A hallmark of divisions like this is that the readers of the apocalyptic work find that they are in the last or next-to-last division of time. Why? Because it is not very encouraging to say, "This terrible persecution will continue on for two more millennia, but eventually God will get around to doing something about it." That message would not help people endure! Apocalyptic cries out, "the end is near, God is about to act, stay faithful just a little longer." So, for example, the *Apocalypse of Weeks* divides all of human history into ten "weeks," seven of which have already passed. Dr. Mitchell Reddish, an authority in apocalyptic literature, observes "The location of the author and his readers in the seventh week, the week of the eschatological crisis, is not accidental. The placement of the readers near the end of world history assures them that the wickedness will not prevail much longer."[22]

What holds all this together is the absolute and total confidence in God's eventual triumph. In apocalyptic literature God always wins. Every time, without fail, God prevails. First century readers did not read Revelation to figure out how things will wind up. Apocalyptic literature is soaked in the enormously comforting certainty of God's judgment. James deSilva writes "Apocalypses such as Revelation, Daniel, and Second Esdras (as well as several lesser known Palestinian Jewish apocalypses) share in common the theme of 'restoration and reversal.'"[23] Yes, it looks bad today, the apocalyptic writer says, but watch what is about to happen in a very short time! For example, in the *Animal Apocalypse*: "And they took all the sealed books and opened those books before the Lord of the sheep. And the Lord called those men... And he said to that man who wrote before him, who was one of the seven white ones—he said to him, Take those seventy shepherds to whom I handed over the sheep.... And behold I saw them all bound, and they all stood before him. And the judgment was held first on the stars, and they were judged and found guilty; and they went to the place of damnation, and were thrown into a deep place, full of fire, burning and full of pillars of fire. And those seventy shepherds were judged and found guilty, and they also were thrown into that abyss of fire" (1 Enoch 90:20-25).

Watch how this plays out in 1 Enoch's *Book of the Watchers*: "And behold! He comes with ten thousand holy ones to execute judgment upon them, and to destroy the impious and to contend with all flesh concerning everything which the sinners and the impious have done and wrought against him" (1 Enoch 1:9). *The War Scroll* has the very same ideas: "For the Master. The rule of War on the unleashing of the attack of the sons of light against the company of the sons of darkness, the army of Satan: against the band of Edom, Moab, and the sons of Ammon, and against the army of the son of the East and the Philistines, and against the bands of the Kittim of Assyria and their allies, the ungodly of the Covenant. The sons of Levi, Judah, and Benjamin, the exiles in the desert, shall battle against them in... all their bands when the exiled sons of light return from the Desert of the Peoples to camp in the Desert of Jerusalem; and after the battle they shall go up from there (to Jerusalem?). The king of the Kittim shall enter into Egypt, and in his time he shall set out in great wrath to wage war against the kings of the north, that his fury may destroy and cut off the horn of Israel. *This shall be a time of salvation for the people of God, an age of dominion for all the members of His company, and of everlasting destruction for all the company of Satan.* The confusion of the sons of Japheth shall be great and Assyria shall fall unsucccoured. The dominion of the Kittim shall come to an end and iniquity shall be vanquished, leaving no remnant; for the sons of darkness there shall be no escape. The sons of righteousness shall shine over all the ends of the earth; they shall go on shining until all the seasons of darkness are consumed and, at the season appointed by God, His exalted greatness shall shine eternally to the peace, blessing, glory, joy, and long life of all the sons of light" (1:1-9).

In the book of Revelation this theme is painted very vividly. From the very outset John sees Jesus as "the Almighty" (1:8). Jesus repeatedly urges the hearers to conquer "as I also conquered and sat down with my Father on His throne" (3:21). The wrath of the Lamb is seen to be all encompassing and devastating. None can stand before it (6:16-17). God's control is seen in marking and sparing certain segments of the population and the earth from His judgment (7:2-3). The book details various judgments upon the earth culminating in the crushing and complete defeat of all of God's enemies, especially the Beast and Babylon (ch. 18, note particularly verse 20). In chapter 19, Jesus rides forth into battle, and John says, "I saw the beast and the kings of the earth with their armies gathered to make war against Him who was sitting on the horse and against His army. And the beast was captured, and with it the false prophet ... these two were thrown alive into the lake of fire that burns with sulfur" (19:19-21). Then even the devil is bound and thrown into a sealed pit (20:1-3). Satan does emerge to cause problems once more, but after attacking God's people again, he and all his helpers are thrown into the lake of fire (20:10) and uninterrupted paradise begins in the wake of God's total victory (chs. 21-22). God absolutely wins. God defeats all evil. God completely triumphs. This is one of apocalyptic literature's most important themes. It is such a key idea in apocalyptic that some have termed it "the apocalyptic cure."[24] The pain of life and its problems were resolved not by "rational argument but by concentration on wonderful revelations."[25]

Perhaps it is important to stop here long enough to deal with the frustrations readers of Revelation in the twenty-first century feel. Many readers of Revelation become exasperated with it because of its dark symbols and visions. If this is all about God's triumph, why doesn't it just come out and say so in straightforward fashion? Yet do not discount how writing in the apocalyptic style holds the reader's attention better, is more exciting and interesting, and thus makes a deeper impression on the reader's heart. A giant mural of battles and bloodshed and white horses and swords and victory—always victory for God and His people—stirs the heart and inspires courage far more than any flat doctrinal pronouncement ever could. Which sentence has more impact? "The wicked will be judged by God and condemned" or "whoever escapes in the war will die by earthquake, and whoever escapes the earthquake will be burned by fire, and whoever escapes the fire will be destroyed by famine" (2 Baruch 70:8). John J. Collins, one of the preeminent scholars in the field of apocalyptic, notes, "the vision of terrible beasts rising out of the sea does not merely give factual information that four kings or kingdoms will arise. It paints a picture of these kingdoms as monstrous eruptions of chaos, in order to convey a sense of terror far beyond anything suggested by the flat statement of the interpretation."[26] The reader does not just understand truth from apocalyptic in his or her head. The reader *feels* its message in his or her very heart and soul.

These very real expectations of apocalyptic literature set the agenda for how we can use Revelation and how to read and understand it today. That can be enormously liberating and helpful as we turn our attention to what apocalyptic does *not* do. Once we quit trying to squeeze out of Revelation what God never intended to put in there (or He would have chosen a different genre) the book begins to make much more sense. It is to this task we will give our attention in chapter five.

V

What Apocalyptic Does Not Do

Despite the complexities of Revelation, it remains one of the most popular books in the Bible. Most Bible class teachers know better than to ask the class, "What should we study?" because such only opens the floor for hard lobbying to study that difficult last book of the Bible. Revelation has also proven to be fertile ground for those who would profit from God's Word by marketing their speculative end times schemes. Hal Lindsey's books were some of the best-selling books in the 1970s with the *Late Great Planet Earth* making terms like "the rapture" and "tribulation" part of the common vernacular to this very day.[27] All this makes Revelation a book with an intimidating reputation.

Yet, by combining our working definition of apocalyptic with a realization of first century expectations of apocalyptic literature we need not be afraid of Revelation. Further, by doing such we can be insulated from conjecture and erroneous supposition. We can use Revelation in a manner consistent with its original purposes and profit from it, because we know what apocalyptic literature is seeking to do. Thus, we also know what it does not do.

Our definition ("A story, written in a time of distress and crisis, that is given by otherworldly beings explaining how God will reverse everything so the righteous will triumph") constrains what we should get from reading an apocalyptic work like Revelation. Its primary function, and what the original readers would have expected from it, would be to emphasize God's sovereign control and to encourage them to faithfulness in a time of crisis and persecution. That is what apocalyptic literature does, and that means, therefore, that apocalyptic runs contrary to the expectation of many Bible students.

For example, apocalyptic literature is not specifically a series of prophecies about the end times. This may stun some people since Revelation is often viewed as the consummate book of prophecy. When the books of the New Testament are placed in their respective divisions, Revelation always appears (by itself) as the New Testament book of prophecy. Many, if not most people, believe that since it is the book of New Testament prophecy, Revelation contains, somewhere in its undecipherable symbols, detailed forecasts of exactly what will happen in our lifetimes as the world comes to an exciting finish and final end. Hal Lindsey once wrote, "To the skeptic who says that Christ is not coming soon, I would ask him to put the book of Revelation in one hand, and the daily newspaper in the other, and then sincerely ask God to show him where we are on His prophetic time-clock."[28] Lindsey penned these words in 1973. So, is God's clock a bit on the slow side? Yet many are sure that all one need do to know the future is read the book of Revelation and watch the cable news network of choice.

However, Revelation is not a prophetic book full of details about the end times because apocalyptic literature does not usually contain detailed prophecy. Apocalyptic literature always says the same thing about the future: evil will get worse and worse and then God will absolutely crush it in complete triumph. In non-inspired apocalyptic literature, one simply does not find it to be brimming with detailed forecasts of the future. There are not wild predictions of empires to come or discussions of watching for astronomical signs. One reason for this (and a handicap that uninspired apocalyptic writers had to deal with) was that predicting the future could undermine the writer's authority when and if those events did not come to pass. Rather than risk being a false prophet (something Mr. Lindsey and his ilk might want to consider), the writers of the apocalyptic material who shaped this genre (largely uninspired men writing between the Testaments) chose to deal in the big theme of God's eventual, certain victory over evil and paint that picture using broad brush strokes. While Revelation's inspired author would have had no problem offering detailed prophecies of the future (near or far), working consistently in this genre precludes such. That is not what readers in New Testament times would have expected from an apocalyptic work.

Some may object that Revelation specifically claims to be a prophecy in Revelation 1:3. John writes there, "Blessed is the one who reads aloud the words of this prophecy... ." Yet all this verse does is recognize that apocalyptic literature is a subset of prophecy. Of course it is prophetic—it is making the ultimate prediction about how the world winds up! But again and again, if one reads apocalyptic literature of every kind from the time before Christ into the Christian era, one will find it is not making the sort of highly specific prophecies that people repeatedly look to find in Revelation. That does not mean that in an inspired book like Revelation we can't find some deviation from the standard patterns of apocalyptic, but to attempt to turn Revelation into a crystal ball by which we can know who will be elected the next President or start watching for the One World Leader is something far from what apocalyptic usually proposes to do. Read apocalyptic literature and about all one will say after watching the evening news or checking some news website is, "Yes, all things are as expected. Evil is getting worse. We must pray God will come soon and fix everything!" To say more is to say more than an apocalyptic book wants to say.

This means that apocalyptic literature like Revelation is not a timetable or calendar by which we can predict the return of Christ. Yet, how many have misused Revelation in this very way? In the spring of 1988 a retired engineer, Edgar Whisenhunt, circulated a booklet titled "88 Reasons Why the Rapture will be in 1988." Much of his material for this prediction was based in his understanding of Revelation. This was also true of his follow-up book "The Final Shout: Rapture Report 1989." As 1990 dawned, Mr. Whisenhunt became part of a long line of people who miserably misunderstood the concept of time in Revelation, to their very public embarrassment.

Without doubt apocalyptic material contains references to time. *The Apocalypse of Weeks* divides history into ten "weeks," seven of which have passed. *2 Baruch* has time divided into periods of black and clear waters, representing time from Adam to the new age: "And when I said this I fell asleep there, and I saw a vision; and lo, a very great cloud was coming up out of the sea. And I kept looking at it. And lo, it was full of waters, white and black ... this happened twelve times" (2 Baruch 53:1, 6). Similar material is found in other apocalyptic works. Careful reading reveals, however, when apocalyptic turns toward discussing time, its interest is not date setting but in something far more important: reinforcing its main themes of God's sovereignty and certain triumph and the need to remain faithful. Adela Yarbro Collins, renowned professor at Yale University, points out that examining all the references to time in Revelation leaves many unanswered questions, lots of overlap, and much uncertainty. Thus, she writes, "the problems which arise when one tries to coordinate these periods of time and to relate them to an absolute chronology show that they were not intended to be interpreted in a literal, chronological way. They do not indicate an interest in precise calculation on the part of the author of Revelation."[29] She goes on to say "it is not the case that the periods of time and numbers in Jewish apocalypses always serve to calculate the end. Their function is usually a symbolic one, helping to create order and meaning in one's perception of history, the world, and life. Rissi's remarks on Revelation, however, are fitting and compatible with the findings of this chapter. The frequent number of people, objects, and events in Revelation make the point by repetition that nothing is random or accidental. Everything is measured and counted. There is a divine plan, all is in God's control, and the outcome will be advantageous to those loyal to God's will as revealed in the book."[30] In other words, by recounting history in set periods of times, the reader is given a feel for a universe that is orderly, where everything happens in its predetermined time. That leads to the major emphasis of time in apocalyptic literature: God is in control. Everything being determined in advance, even how long evil people and nations will be allowed to persecute God's people, shows without doubt the control of an all-powerful God. All history is in God's hands. So, yes, it does appear that the world has careened off its axis and is hurtling out of control into darkness and more troubles for the godly. But apocalyptic literature jumps in to say, "Wait! What is happening now is not the whole story. God is in control. God rules over everything, including time."

As apocalyptic literature is making that point, it is standard operating procedure to place the readers very close to the end when God does come. This is what most time references in apocalyptic writings are about. They do not invite calculation.

There is no reason to add or multiply numbers in all sorts of remarkably creative ways in order to derive dates. Nor do they ask to be written in a day planner or establish a timetable for world events. Most time references simply say, as John Collins writes, "the turning point is at hand."[31] The key words of apocalyptic literature are "soon" and "quickly." "Say to him in my name, 'Hide yourself, and reveal to him the end *which is coming*, for the whole earth will be destroyed, and a deluge *is about to come on* all the earth'" (1 Enoch 10:2). This same emphasis is found in Revelation. John writes of things that "must soon take place" (1:1) for the "time is near" (1:3). God "has sent his angel to show his servants what must soon take place" (22:6) because Jesus is coming soon, an idea repeated no less than three times (22:7, 12, 20). In apocalyptic literature the only time that matters is *now* because the readers are so close to the end and the faithful need to hold on. A future that will take place hundreds of years from now is not discussed in apocalyptic. How could it be? Since God is coming very soon to begin the new world, it would be foolish for apocalyptic writings to prophesy or set dates for all sorts of far-distant world events, tyrants and wars. According to apocalyptic literature, all of that will be gone very soon.

Finally, it is important to understand that an apocalyptic work is not attempting to develop finely detailed doctrinal truths in its use of symbols and metaphors. Examining the apocalyptic literature available in New Testament times reveals that it is not hiding impressive truths in tiny details. Instead, and generally speaking, apocalyptic literature deals in big, dramatic scenes that deeply impress the reader with the horror of evil or the awesomeness of God. There is little subtlety about the symbolism, what is happening or where the action is headed. Yet it is quite common for commentaries and books about Revelation to begin with detailed charts making certain "every claw on every paw" is accounted for and allegorized as standing for something crucially important. Of course, such interpretations are usually rather arbitrary. They come from the mind of the commentator and what he or she thinks topaz represents or what the color green means. Apocalyptic does not dabble in such fine points, choosing instead to trumpet very loudly its one main message. To understand more of how that works, we need to watch how apocalyptic literature uses its own symbols and visionary creatures. Get ready—in the next chapter we will meet sea beasts, fiery mountains, mighty angels, and more!

VI
Imagery in Apocalyptic Literature

While Revelation is easily one of the most popular books of the New Testament, at the same time it is also one of the least understood books of the New Testament. Gallons of ink, reams of paper, and hours of study have not brought everyone to a quick understanding of its message. What is the problem? Without doubt, it is the imagery and symbolic language of Revelation that throws the reader into confusion and despair. What do we make of locusts with scorpion tails (9:3ff), wanton harlots (17:1), or black horses (6:5)?

Too often Bible students have let these exciting and mysterious images distract them from what apocalyptic literature like Revelation is really trying to accomplish. Let us take a look at how apocalyptic in first century times used such symbols so that we can better understand what to do with Revelation's vivid imagery.

If one reads apocalyptic material from the first century times, one truth becomes quickly apparent that has enormous implications for how we treat apocalyptic symbols: not everything in an apocalyptic vision has to mean something. Of course, it is very common today for a commentary or Bible class teacher to spin fantastic tales from the most minor detail in Revelation. This writer once heard a preacher announce the total population of heaven to be 100,000,000 because Revelation 5:11 said the throne of God was surrounded by ten thousand times ten thousand creatures! The preacher had simply done the math to deduce this astounding doctrinal point. Many people make the ten toes of the statue in Daniel 2 (described in Daniel 2:41-42) to be a clear sign of ten kings or ten nations that are bound together in a confederation. Read Daniel 2 carefully, however, and you will find no mention of ten toes. The statue has "feet and toes" but the number ten is not ever specified, nor is anything made of the number ten. One wonders if an interpretation of the statue that hinged on the number two (because the statue had two ankles) would be as widely received or believed! Yet there is just as much basis for counting ankles as there is for calculating toes. This kind of close scrutiny of details that are not singled out in the text is all too common in the interpretation of the Bible's apocalyptic literature.

Yet an examination of apocalyptic literature available in the first century shows that this is precisely the wrong direction to go with Revelation. Instead of getting out an electron microscope to minutely look at every detail or multiply every number, what Revelation really calls for is the reader to stand back for a panoramic view. Apocalyptic is not, as often supposed, a highly detailed diagram with crucial information hidden in the fine print. In fact, apocalyptic literature is not a diagram or doctrinal treatise at all. Instead, it is much more akin to a huge mural. For example, in the *Apocalypse of Abraham* we read of a strong angel who is described like this, "the appearance of his body was like sapphire, and the look of his countenance like chrysolite, and the hair of his head like snow, and the turban on his head like the appearance of the rainbow, and the clothing of his garments like purple, and a golden scepter was in his right hand" (11:8).[32] No effort is made by the author to do anything with these colors. Sapphire, purple, and chrysolite are not assigned any special significance, nor is the rainbow's meaning discussed. None of those colors are ever mentioned again in the book. Instead of dissecting the appearance of the angel, the text focuses on what this character is saying. The colors simply serve to appropriately costume this dramatic figure so that the reader knows this character is important and will listen to what he says. But again, nothing special or spectacular is made out of every detail of what he wears, or any particular point of his appearance.

This is a consistent pattern in apocalyptic literature. Notice the throne scene of 1 Enoch 14, which is highly reminiscent of Revelation 4-5. "Violently agitated and trembling, I fell upon my face. In the vision I looked. And behold there was another habitation more spacious than the former, every entrance to which was open before me, erected in the midst of a vibrating flame. *So greatly did it excel in all points, in glory, in magnificence, and in magnitude, that it is impossible to describe to you either the splendor or the extent of it.* Its floor was on fire; above were lightnings and agitated stars, while its roof exhibited a blazing fire. Attentively I surveyed it, and saw that it contained an exalted throne; the appearance of which was like that of frost; while its circumference resembled the orb of the brilliant sun; and there was the voice of the cherubim. From underneath this mighty throne rivers of flaming fire issued. To look upon it was impossible. One great in glory sat upon it: Whose robe was brighter than the sun, and whiter than snow. No angel was capable of penetrating to view the face of Him, the Glorious and the Effulgent; nor could any mortal behold Him. A fire was flaming around Him" (1 Enoch 14:14-22).[33] Rather than urge us to fixate on every particular point, such as what it means to have fire on

God's floor and roof or what a throne the color of frost signifies, the author plainly states, "it is impossible to describe to you" its splendor, and so he describes it as best he can, an amazing scene that focuses all attention on God. The details of what surrounds that throne scene are unimportant and need to be left for what they are: details. They are window dressing— essential to set the scene but not important on their own. The author is clearly doing all this descriptive work so we will focus on the One on the throne, not on the throne's surroundings!

Apocalyptic by its nature is full of vivid descriptions of beasts, animals, otherworldly beings, weather, and events. *The Apocalypse of Zephaniah* has angels with leopard faces and tusks (4:3)! 1 Enoch 90:2 mentions all manner of birds, such as eagles, vultures, and ravens that come and attack God's people. These varied and colorful details are essential to making apocalyptic what it is: dramatic, inspiring, overpowering, and memorable. Yet in none of these cases does the apocalyptic writer hide significant meaning in such details.

Another example reinforces this crucial point. In 4 Ezra 5:610 we read: "But if the Most High grants that you live, you shall see it thrown into confusion after the third period; and the sun shall suddenly shine forth at night, and the moon during the day. Blood shall drip from wood, and the stone shall utter its voice; the peoples shall be troubled, and the stars shall fall. And one shall reign whom those who dwell on earth do not expect, and the birds shall fly away together; and the sea of Sodom shall cast up fish; and one whom the many do not know shall make his voice heard by night, and all shall hear his voice. There shall be chaos also in many places, and fire shall often break out, and the wild beasts shall roam beyond their haunts, and menstruous women shall bring forth monsters. And salt waters shall be found in the sweet, and all friends shall conquer one another; then shall reason hide itself, and wisdom shall withdraw into its chamber, and it shall be sought by many but shall not be found, and unrighteousness and unrestraint shall increase on earth." What is the meaning of each of these expressions: "blood shall drip from wood" or "stones will talk" or "menstruous women shall bring forth monsters?" The writer tells us plainly what he means: "you shall see ... confusion" and "wisdom will withdraw." In other words, there will be a time of tremendous bedlam and turmoil. The writer of *4 Ezra* is not inviting us to speculate about what astronomical phenomena would cause the sun to shine at night or make birds fly away together or cause women to give birth to monsters. He is instead painting a dramatic portrait of barbarous times. The point he wants to make is not in the details but is in all the details working together to emphasize the chaos and anarchy of the times. In fact, over-analyzing those details obscures his meaning. To use a word-picture to explain this idea (as apocalyptic writers do) we must realize that if we stop to examine each individual petal on every flower we will miss what we ought to be seeing: we are standing in a flower garden! It is the overall picture that matters in apocalyptic imagery, not the individual details.

Does this mean that nothing in apocalyptic literature ever "stands for" or is analogous to something? Of course not. In *4 Ezra* an eagle appears and is clearly to be identified with the Roman Empire, and the lion that defeats that eagle is obviously the Messiah. How do we know this? Because *4 Ezra* says so! "The eagle which you saw coming up from the sea is the fourth kingdom which appeared in a vision to your brother Daniel... *This is the interpretation*: It is these whom the Most High has kept for the eagle's end; this was the reign which was brief and full of tumult, as you have seen. And as for the lion whom you saw rousing up out of the forest and roaring and speaking to the eagle and reproving him for his unrighteousness, and as for all his words that you have heard this is the Messiah whom the Most High has kept until the end of days, who will arise from the posterity of David, and will come and speak to them; he will denounce them for their ungodliness and for their wickedness, and will cast up before them their contemptuous dealings" (4 Ezra 12:11, 30-31).

Explanation sections like this are very common in apocalyptic writings. Ironically, while the word "apocalypse" means an uncovering or unveiling, apocalyptic authors realized that apocalyptic—with its symbols and signs—might veil or cover up the message. So, they made sure it was not covered up by having the main character ask the angel who is showing the vision "what does this mean?" or "what am I looking at?" Alternatively, the angel will ask the main character "Do you know who or what this is?" Such interpretation sections occur in many apocalypses. For example, in 2 Baruch 13 the writer is told, "You shall serve as witness" so that when people ask why God has destroyed the holy city he can give the correct theological answer. As the visions in *2 Baruch* continue, the writer asks more questions and is told "I will explain these things to you as well" (42:1). In Chapter 56 the heavenly being says, "you have asked the Most High to reveal to you the interpretation of the vision you have seen and I have been sent to tell you" (verse 1). What follows then is a clear explanation of the vision of the black and white waters and who is who in that vision. Towards the close of the book the angel says, "Since the interpretation of this vision has been given to you as you asked…" (76:1).

Again, in the specific interpretations and explanations that apocalyptic material contains, everything does not stand for something and every detail is not given significance. Every detail of the beasts or animals or weather phenomena is not laboriously pulled out so that something can be made of it. Instead, invariably the main characters and main actions are explained in broad and straightforward ways. Terrible beasts are evil empires on the loose. Weird events show evil increasing. God's throne room is magnificent and incredible, underscoring His sovereign rule and power. Detailed questions that we might like to ask, such as "Why is the dragon red?" are not treated at all. Thus apocalyptic writers kept their audiences from zooming in too tightly on the image and missing the big picture.

1 Enoch 24 provides a good example of this. "Enoch" sees seven high mountains with beautiful stones and a fragrant tree in the midst of the mountains that smells wonderful. What does this mean? The reader does not have to wonder nor try to assign some esoteric meaning to it. Enoch is told, "This high mountain you saw, whose summit is like the throne of the Lord, is the throne where the Holy and Great One, the Lord of Glory, the Eternal King, will sit … and this beautiful fragrant tree… will be given to the righteous and humble. From its fruit life will be given to the chosen" (1 Enoch 25:2-6). Interestingly, in

all these explanations the tree is said to be planted in the north (25:5) and from it rivers run south (26:6) but nothing is made of any of these directions, and they are not allegorized, nor are they identified with any country nor is any specific application of those directions made. This is the very kind of thing that students today fixate on in Revelation, but here we see such details are simply part of the scenery and are not given any kind of interpretation full of hidden meaning. It is clear that when one watches how apocalyptic literature uses symbols and visionary happenings, it does not make anything of its details, nor nuance them to make fine doctrinal points the reader might miss. That simply does not happen in apocalyptic literature.

Examples like this can be multiplied. If the reader of the *Apocalypse of Zephaniah* is wondering about those leopardfaced angels with tusks, those questions are quickly answered. The text says, "when I saw them, I was afraid. I said unto that angel who walked with me, 'Of what sort are these?' He said unto me, 'These are the servants of all creation who come to the souls of ungodly men and bring them and leave them in this place [eternal hell, mdr]'" (4:5-6).[34] The explanation given is that these angels have a tough job and so obviously a leopard-faced angel with tusks is necessary to do that kind of work! Note again, however, nothing specific or special is made of their tusks or leopard faces. That is just part of the "make up" for a fierce angel. In 1 Enoch 46 "Enoch" asks about the dramatic figure he sees and then records that the angel, "who went with me and showed me all the secrets about that Son of Man, who he was…

said to me, 'This is the Son of Man....'" Again, there is no need to guess or speculate. In the *Testament of Abraham*, "Abraham" asks the angel "My lord Prince, who is this wondrous judge...?" (13:1), and he is told in no uncertain terms that he is seeing Abel. In the *Apocalypse of Peter* there is a scene that looks like the Transfiguration. So, "Peter" asks, "My Lord who is this?" and is told it is Moses and Elias (16:1). In 5 Ezra 2:44, "Ezra" asks "who are these my Lord?" and the angel tells him he is seeing the righteous.

All of these illustrations demonstrate how it is common for apocalyptic literature to explain itself. About the time the reader is wondering, "What or who is that?" the leading character inquires from God or the angel showing him the vision, and then the leading character (and the reader) receive an explanation. This means if the apocalypse does not stop and tell us what we are seeing, we may not want to make too much of what is before us. The author of the apocalypse did not, so why would we? Revelation uses explanation sections in exactly the same way.

In Revelation 4 the throne room of God is described with all kinds of details, such as various colors and who surrounds the throne, and that there is a sea in front of it (4:1-6). In the midst of all of this, we read that "before the throne were burning seven torches of fire, which are the seven spirits of God." This is the only detail that is given any specific mention or interpretation. Why then do so many commentaries and books on Revelation contain an extensive catalogue of what every color stands for or add and subtract the twenty-four elders before the throne to get all kinds of meanings, such as the twelve patriarchs plus the twelve apostles? If John didn't invest meaning in those details, why must we? When Revelation wants us to know what something means, it never hesitates to make it abundantly clear what is happening. In Revelation 5 a creature comes forward to take and open the sealed book. Who is this creature? "And one of the elders said to me, 'Weep no more; behold, the Lion of the tribe of Judah, the Root of David, has conquered, so that he can open the scroll and its seven seals'" (5:6). That is pretty hard to miss! So it goes throughout Revelation. In chapter seven it is important that the readers know the identity of the persons who are sealed on their foreheads. Do we have to guess? No. "Then one of the elders addressed me, saying, 'Who are these, clothed in white robes, and from where have they come?' I said to him, 'Sir, you know.' And he said to me, 'These are the ones coming out of the great tribulation. They have washed their robes and made them white in the blood of the Lamb'" (7:13-14).

In the same way, much has been made of the fierce locusts of Revelation 9 with their hair and teeth and breastplates and stinging tails. Those who find today's news in Revelation see attack helicopters or other military hardware in these descriptions, as if John was unable to write clearly about future aircraft or weaponry or as if that would encourage first century Christians. However, John makes no use of the details of their description, just showing us that they bring woe and misery to the earth. If that is all John makes of the hairy locusts, why are some sure they are really teaching the message of Revelation when they do more? Like other apocalyptic literature, Revelation will tell us what we need to know to grasp its message. The astute reader will note passages like 14:8-13; 16:14; 17:1, 7, 15ff and 20:2 that make plain the action and what its significance is. Apocalyptic literature wants to reveal truth, not cover it up— and it will work to make plain what the reader must know.

In fairness, it must be noted that sometimes there is no explanation section to be found. However, this is often the case because the imagery is so obvious. How hard was it for the readers of *4 Ezra* to know the eagle that burned down Jerusalem was Rome since the readers knew that Roman armies marched bearing eagle standards? In the *Animal Apocalypse* a bull becomes a man and builds for himself a large boat, after which there is a huge flood and all the wicked animals drown (89:1-9). It does not take much effort to recognize that the author is describing Noah, does it? The symbolism of the *Sibylline Oracles* makes much of the common belief that Nero had died and then revived, or come back to life, but it is easy to see what the writer is pointing to because this "great king of Rome" murders his mother and otherwise acts exactly as Nero had (see Sib Or 3:6370; Sib Or 5:137-154). It is just not that hard to figure out because the author wants us to understand whom he is referencing. Similarly, recognizing Rome and Roman rulers in the vision of the beast in Revelation 13 is patently obvious.

Apocalyptic literature wants us to understand and so regularly explains itself or simply makes its message too plain to miss.

By now it is apparent this chapter takes a profoundly different approach to Revelation's symbols and visions. By watching how apocalyptic material uses imagery, we have come to realize that allegorizing Revelation is not only not necessary, it actually is a barrier to genuine understanding. Hopefully this relieves the pressure to make something of everything in Revelation, or find some historical equivalent to all that is shown to John. That freedom alone should make the reader more comfortable with Revelation.

Remember, as a rule, symbolism that matters, that the author wants the readers to understand, will either be so obvious as to be impossible to miss or will be directly explained in some kind of question and answer format. Again, it is crucial to realize that in explanation sections very rarely, if ever, does the writer make use of some minute detail and invest it with great significance. We are made much more comfortable with Revelation by simply realizing that what so many think they must do in Revelation—parse every detail in high definition—is not done in apocalyptic literature.

One writer has said that apocalyptic is not governed by logic because it is poetry.[35] Never is the truth of this statement better seen than when studying apocalyptic imagery. As long as modern-day readers try to stuff Revelation full of today's breaking headlines, spinning subtle shades of meaning onto every vision and metaphor to arrive at their preconceived notions, the real message of Revelation will elude us. Going closely with that, as long as Bible class teachers and commentators are praised and deemed "more spiritual" or "really deep" based on how much they can read into every detail of Revelation, the actual message of Revelation will be lost.

Apocalyptic literature is about big themes (such as the ultimate victory of God over evil). It is very black and white in its worldview and perspective. It divides the entire universe into "for" and "against" camps. One either serves God or serves the devil. To convey the messages of exactly where the reader needs to stand and how essential perseverance and faithfulness are, it does not invest every claw on every paw with meaning. Forcing into apocalyptic literature all kinds of "higher meaning" was certainly not how apocalyptic literature was used in New Testament times. Delightfully, once we stop trying to make everything stand for something and to explain every beast and cataclysmic judgment that occurs, we are then free to let Revelation say what it has always wanted to say: "be faithful unto death and you will receive the crown of life" (2:10). In the next chapter we will build on this understanding using a visual metaphor common in our times that provides us tremendous help in better understanding ancient apocalyptic literature.

VII

Misusing Apocalyptic
Going to the Movies in Revelation

Americans have a long-standing love affair with movies. Millions of Americans see movies every week. Either by making a trip to a theater (with its wonderful aroma of popcorn), or by renting a DVD to play in high definition on the home theater screen, or perhaps by simply flipping on the television, or increasingly by downloading it via the Internet, Americans cannot get enough movie entertainment.

Interestingly, while each year some truly original films are produced, many of the movies we all enjoy can easily be pigeonholed into a specific type of movie. Moviegoers commonly talk about "chick flicks" or "spy thrillers" or "slasher films." This is genre talk. People may not realize it but they are designating various movies by their type or kind, and that is exactly what genre is about. Each of these different genres or kinds of movies involves its own plot line, way of developing characters, vocabulary, and expectations from the audience. For example, everyone knows how a classic "chick flick" works and what we will see if we attend (or are dragged to) such a movie. At such movies the good guy and the girl will eventually end up together. There is never any question about it. If the movie is a "slasher film," we know that the killer will be everywhere at once, and that anyone who wanders away from the main group will certainly be murdered. We also know that after the killer is terminated he will, somehow, arise from the fire, fall, or whatever killed him, to almost get the hero one last time, causing everyone to jump out of his seat one more time.

Some of these expectations are so obvious that movie critics speak of "formula movies." Formula movies go by the book, simply fulfilling all the expectations of that type or genre of film. The director seems to have checked off all the expectations for the kind of movie he is making and then dropped it into theaters (where sadly, it usually does very well at the box office). Other movies have been successful by taking apart or flaunting the conventions of the day. DreamWorks' *Shrek* films have received wide acclaim largely because they gleefully tear apart the conventional Disney fairy tales that we have all seen so many times. Both the way Americans talk about movies and how they enjoy movies that "break the rules" shows clearly that Americans know all about movie genre.

That understanding of genre can help students of Revelation. Perhaps like no other book of the Bible, Revelation is most like a movie. Can anyone really imagine making a movie of 2 Corinthians? That would be difficult! Of course, movies have been made from the four Gospels and that works fairly well to show the action parts of Christ's life. However, such films are usually tremendously unsatisfying because a huge part of Jesus' life was His preaching and teaching. Two hours of Jesus discoursing on the nature of the kingdom of heaven does not translate well to film. In contrast to that, think about what a movie Revelation could be! In fact, many readers of Revelation will even express a desire for someone to paint the scenes of the book. "I wish I had some pictures to look at as I read this!" is a common lament from first-timers reading Revelation. Such is understandable because Revelation (and apocalyptic literature in general) is such a visual genre. Revelation calls for its readers to see in their mind's eye tremendous events, astonishing characters, and incredible action. The whole book brims with seeing language:

"The revelation of Jesus Christ, which God gave him *to show* to his servants the things that must soon take place" (1:1). "Write *what you see* in a book and send it to the seven churches" (1:11).

"After this I *looked*, and behold, a door standing open in heaven! And the first voice, which I had heard speaking to me like a trumpet, said, 'Come up here, and *I will show you* what must take place after this'" (4:1).

"Then one of the seven angels who had the seven bowls came and said to me, 'Come, *I will show you* the judgment of the great prostitute who is seated on many waters'" (17:1).

"Then came one of the seven angels who had the seven bowls full of the seven last plagues and spoke to me, saying, 'Come, *I will show you* the Bride, the wife of the Lamb'" (21:9).

Perhaps we should not read Revelation as much as we should try to see it. If Spielberg or Lucas are looking for a challenge, for something that would stretch their computers and all their movie-making wizardry to the limit, they should try filming the book of Revelation. If someone did so they might make the book accessible and understandable in a way no commentator has ever been able to do. Explaining Revelation is one thing. Showing it is something else. The repeated emphasis on "seeing" and "showing" bears much thought for students who are determined to understand Revelation the way its original audience did.

Indeed, thinking of Revelation as a movie, especially for a people who are so comfortable with movies, can be tremendously helpful to knowing how to handle apocalyptic literature. There are rules for movie genre that everyone knows. Audiences would be stunned at a "chick flick" if the good guy was about to propose to his love interest, only to suddenly see him assassinated by ninjas. We know, however, how those kinds of movies work. We understand the genre, and we know that ninjas do not normally appear in "chick flicks!" So, what are the "rules" for an apocalyptic "movie?" In some ways they are very much like the rules for watching our 21st century films.

For example, what of people who try to make a movie into something it isn't? Granted, there are movies that are metaphorical or have a definite agenda and message. What is so tiresome is the guy who wants to believe he is really educated and cultured and so can see a "deep meaning" in every movie. The *Star Wars* movies are very popular and very beloved (with the obvious exception of JarJar Binks). Yet some avant-garde movie critic who offers that in his lofty opinion *Star Wars* is a metaphor for how the enslaved lower classes have to fight Big Industry to win their freedom will not get much of a hearing. Perhaps that is *Star Wars'* message, but such does not seem very apparent to most people. To most folks *Star Wars* is just fun. It is a good old-fashioned bad guys versus good guys "shoot'em up" set in outer space. Trying to discern some deeper message in the movie ruins it.

Yet, this is the very thing that happens to Revelation. Upon a first reading, Revelation appears to be offering help and comfort to its first century readers. The calls for faithfulness under the pressure of persecution and the call to hold out because God will vindicate the faithful occur through the book (see 2:10; 6:9-11; 7:14; 9:20-21; 12:17; 13:10b; 16:15; 17:14; 21:3-4, 7-8; 22:3-5, 12-15, 20). This fits exactly with how apocalyptic literature was read and used in New Testament times. Is everyone content to let Revelation have that obvious meaning? Absolutely not. Instead of saying, "This was for those people in that time and helped them," people feel obligated to somehow force it to be a prophecy of something happening in our day. Many interpreters of Revelation seem to forget that "the language of apocalypses is not descriptive, referential, newspaper language, but the *expressive* language of poetry, which uses symbols and imagery to articulate a sense or feeling about the world."[36] The problem with making this contemporary is, of course, that "this approach ignores the historical and social matrix out of which apocalyptic literature arose. Apocalyptic writers addressed the situation of their own time, attempting to offer hope and encouragement to their readers who were in distress."[37] Why can't *Star Wars* be just good fun? Why try to make it into more than it is? Similarly, why can't Revelation be what it says it is: a message for first century times about the first century world?

Closely accompanying this difficulty is the terrible problem of wanting to autopsy the movie. Imagine for a moment a Western movie. What color hats do the bad guys wear? We all know that the bad guys wear black hats. Why do the bad guys wear black hats? No one knows. They just do. That is standard headgear for villains in Western movies. If someone was to assign some deep meaning to black hats in Western movies, we would quickly recognize how artificial and forced such an interpretation is. If they went further and began to analyze and assign meaning to hatbands or belt buckles, we would be even less impressed. Western movies use stock images. That kind of imagery is not full of hidden details or meanings. Cutting it all apart with a scalpel and assigning a meaning to every piece would ruin the movie. Doing an autopsy on *Big Jake* kills the movie.

Amazingly, making the same mistake with Revelation often results in praise instead of rebuke. Commentaries that can come up with some correspondence between the minutest details of a vision and today's news are viewed as having special insight. The more a Bible class teacher can interpret or allegorize in Revelation, the more the class is impressed with how learned this teacher is. Sadly, a Bible class teacher that cannot make everything in Revelation fit something will often find unhappiness in the class. There may even be a general feeling that the class is not really getting everything in the book. James Efird, professor emeritus at Duke University, rightly notes "Some interpreters want to find meaning in every detail of the vision, but this seems to be going much too far, making the visionary scene into some sort of tightly knit allegory... [some of apocalyptic] is 'window dressing' to enhance the overall impact of the message."[38] J. Ramsey Michaels, a prolific writer and scholar, joins in that warning as he says "Caird rightly warns us that 'to compile such a catalogue is to unweave the rainbow. John uses his allusions not as a code in which each symbol requires separate and exact translation, but rather for their evocative and emotive power.'"[39] Apocalyptic literature compares very well to our modern-day movies in this respect because apocalyptic writers work very much with stock images, as in our movies. One does not question or dissect the stock image of an evil beast, or mighty angel, any more than one would dissect why ObiWan Kenobi's light saber glows blue while Darth Vader's glows red. Putting visual mediums, like apocalyptic literature, on the autopsy table to cut out every detail and examine it with microscopic precision destroys them.

It is also important that students of Revelation realize that apocalyptic does not have interchangeable parts. If one sees a Western movie in which the bad guys (black hats and all) are attempting to rob the stagecoach, that viewer probably will not assume the next time he or she sees a Western that the bad guys will try to hold up the stagecoach again. We would recognize the bad guys (because they have black hats on) and would assume they are up to no good, but would easily understand in this new movie they will be involved in some new nefarious caper.

This is the very error that dispensational premillenialism makes. Reading the stuff that Ryrie or Lindsey or Walvoord and their disciples put out is roughly akin to staring at a patchwork quilt. They run all over the Bible, grabbing part of this vision and stitching it to that vision and then taking the whole thing and fastening it onto an entirely different book of the Bible. By running the sewing machine long enough, they finally produce something that might make it look (if one closes one eye tightly and squints with the other) like the book of Revelation could be talking about the European economic consortium or ecoterrorism or whatever else is in today's news.

It never seems to occur to people that Daniel might be written for Daniel's audience, and that Jesus in Matthew 24 was talking to an entirely different group of people, and John is writing to yet another entirely separate group of people in

Revelation *and that each message must be allowed to stand on its own*. Adela Collins writes of the common idea "compare Scripture with Scripture" (meaning one passage in the Bible can be explained by another passage) noting that "responsible interpretation of a text from another time and place requires that the text be interpreted in terms of its original historical context."[40] While it seems hard to argue with the idea that Scripture interprets Scripture, there are limitations to it. For example, while Paul uses leaven as a metaphor for sin (1 Corinthians 5:7), Jesus uses leaven to describe the working of the kingdom of God (Matthew 13:33). No responsible Bible student would decide that leaven is *always* evil and develop a complex list of rules about buying bread today based on the requirements to put leaven out of the house for Passover (Exodus 12:19) or what Jesus says about it in Mark 8:15. The way Scripture uses leaven as a metaphor does not allow such. Comparing metaphors from all over the Bible must be done carefully.

Similarly, we must proceed with great caution when comparing apocalyptic imagery from one part of the Bible with similar imagery in another part of the Bible. One cannot simply assume that because there is a beast in Daniel that it is the very same beast, doing the same evil deeds in the same evil way, as the beast one is now reading about in Revelation. That won't work with apocalyptic literature. For example, several apocalyptic pieces use as their villain the people known as the "Kittim." The *War Scroll* says the "Kittim" will help the "Sons of Darkness, the army of Belial" (column 1). In the *War Scroll* the reference is clearly to the Romans. However, 1 Maccabees says Alexander the Great came from the land of the Kittim (8:5).[41] Alexander came from Greece, not Rome. There are other references to the Kittim being from Greece. Daniel 11, however, uses the Kittim as Roman. In short, the Kittim do not have one settled use or meaning. Different writers use the term to reference the bad guy of their time. To go to 1 Maccabees to identify the "Kittim" as the Greeks and then shove that definition into Daniel 11 will not work. The parts and symbols of apocalyptic are not interchangeable. John Collins reminds us that apocalyptic writers "may well allow loose ends and even contradictions to stand in their work... it is not governed by the principles of Aristotlean logic."[42] Using the term "contradictions" to describe Bible material may press readers' hot buttons, but be assured, while unable to speak for Collins, this author is certainly not implying the inspired Scriptures contain any errors or contradictions. In apocalyptic material, however, imagery and metaphor may not always line up to suit our 21st century kind of thinking with its emphasis on linear, orderly time and logic. For example, in Revelation 7:15-17 a temple and tabernacle are present in heaven, but in Revelation 21:22-23 it is said no temple is necessary because God and the Lamb are the temple. This is not a contradiction. It is simply two different word pictures emphasizing the blessedness of being in God's presence, from two different perspectives. Yet this well illustrates how comfortable apocalyptic writers are in painting vivid (even wild) scenes that sometimes contrast with other scenes already painted, all done to point to the same "big picture" truths. Apocalyptic literature's original readers would not have been troubled by this or derailed by it, and we must not be either. Perhaps the idea of Revelation as a mural helps again here. In ancient battle murals the conquering army would appear in several panels, first drawn up in battle, then in the middle of the mural conquering the enemy, and then finally showing the enemy being led away in defeat and disgrace. No one would look at the mural and say, "It contradicts itself! It shows the army in three places at the same time." That is not how the mural works. An overemphasis on rigid literalism would ruin it, and likewise will ruin an apocalyptic "mural." Further, none of Revelation's readers (even with their familiarity of the Old Testament) would have tried to make sense of it by poring over Ezekiel and Daniel to find some similar figure which would lead to the "discovery" or "decoding" of John's real meaning in the book of Revelation. Each apocalyptic "movie" must be allowed to stand on its own.

Finally, and perhaps most important of all, Revelation, like all movies, should be "watched" in one sitting. There has been much talk in this book about reading Revelation like its first readers did. Yet the first people to receive Revelation did not read it at all. It *was read* to them. Imagine then an assembly at Sardis. The church is gathered together. An elder stands up and announces, "We have received the scroll from Thyatira that we have been hearing about. It is from the apostle John. He has much to say to us about the troubling times we live in." The elder opens the scroll and then begins reading. After reading for a minute or so, he stops and says "Well, that's far enough. Let's stop and talk about what is being said here. Brother Hermes, what did you get out of that?" Weeks go by. At every meeting only a tiny portion of the scroll is read and discussed. A year or more passes before the end of the scroll even begins to be in sight.

Of course, such would never happen. The church would be eager to hear *all* that John had to say. They would never be content to spend weeks analyzing the introductory vision of Jesus and then spend weeks more on the messages to Ephesus, Smyrna, Pergamum, and Thyatira. They would want to know *now* what John had said to and about them. Once they got past the messages to the churches, how could anyone stop reading when John began to describe the incredible visions he saw in heaven of the war between good and evil? Further, if Revelation is a circular letter as many believe, then the churches mentioned after Sardis would be waiting to receive it. They would be eager to receive the scroll. They would be quite unhappy to hear they would not be receiving it until Sardis had completed its exhaustive three-year study of the book!

Yet how do many people and Bible classes study Revelation?

Many classes are on the three-year exhaustive plan. Much of this is caused by the thinking that every detail in every verse demands in-depth explanation. Journeying all over the Bible to find every occurrence of the figures found in Revelation occupies more time. Reading into the text current events and somehow making the text analogous to what goes on today takes even longer. The result? A book that should, in a few readings, powerfully paint a picture of God's sovereignty and triumph over evil is reduced to an impotent bunch of disjointed oddities and weird symbols. The book's great central message is completely lost.

If a group watched *The Princess Bride* in eight-minute bits, stopping after each segment to discuss what everyone had seen, would it be any surprise that what the group got out of *The Princess Bride* was very different than what the original audience got when they watched it all in one sitting in a theater? There would be all kinds of connections and important ideas missed simply because by the time the group viewed the end of the movie it had been so long since they had seen its beginning. Do we do any better when take a few verses of Revelation in every Bible class, stretching out the study of the book over months and years?

Revelation is only twenty-two chapters long. It is not too long for a group to read it aloud all in one or two sessions. Those who try this approach consistently find the book suddenly becomes very different and is much more manageable. When we are liberated from the burden of stopping to make something out of every detail in every passage, we can read it fairly quickly. Then the book comes together in a new and wonderful way, as its themes stand out clearly. What it was meant to do it can do, while so many of the interpretive games people play with Revelation get left behind. Instead of fearing we missed something in such a quick reading, we find we gained everything. Trying to read as much of Revelation in one sitting as we can is a marvelous way to "watch" John's great movie. Doing so means we are reading it like the Christians in the first century read it, and we are using it the way apocalyptic literature was meant to be used. And that means we will be getting from it what they did. Surely that must be the goal of our efforts in reading and studying Revelation.

VIII
To Sum Up

A book with a title like *Understanding Apocalyptic Literature: A Guide to the Book of Revelation* makes a big promise to its readers. Hopefully this book has made good on that promise and its readers are better equipped to understand John's great apocalypse. With that increase in knowledge there should also be an increase in confidence. By learning about the genre of apocalyptic literature, the book of Revelation begins to appear in an entirely new light. Some might even dare to suggest that it even looks manageable! Revelation *can* be understood, something the book plainly announces at its outset as its express intention (1:3). That means that while a verse-by-verse commentary of Revelation is far beyond the scope of this volume, an excellent way to conclude this book would be to pull together the principles we have learned about interpreting apocalyptic literature. Doing that lets us see where we have been and points us toward future studies in Revelation with new hope.

Perhaps no principle is more important in dealing with Revelation than letting less be more. There are countless novel and unique approaches to this unusual book. Almost anything and nearly everything has been found in John's visions by some interpreters. What is disappointing about this is not so much the harebrained ideas read into the book of Revelation but that so many students give credence to such. In some ways it almost seems the crazier and more intricately detailed the interpretations are, the more people are impressed with the supposed depth of insight such reveals. Yet no other book of the Bible is so treated. For example, the infamous Jesus Seminar minutely scrutinizes the Gospels to decide the source of every saying and every happening. With "form criticism" and "redaction criticism" cranked up to warp speed, the Seminar minutely examines the texts of the Gospels and then holds forth with its findings. Not surprisingly they usually end up saying that only a few fragments here and there are genuine. However, most people give their work little interest or credibility. The Gospels continue to be widely accepted as authentic accounts of Jesus' life and teachings. There is just something about the very methodology of turning Scripture inside out and x-raying it in a highly technical, academically obscure fashion that says to most people, "That is a hoax with an agenda behind it." The Bible, if it is what it claims to be, ought to be accessible to ordinary people reading it in ordinary ways. If one has to have a Ph.D. and a working understanding of New Testament Greek (with a side order of Aramaic) to understand Scripture, then God has utterly failed to communicate with most of humanity. Thus, most people look for a fairly straight-forward, common sense kind of approach to the Bible throughout sixty-five of its sixty-six books. If someone announced Judges was an allegory and Deborah was not a real person but instead represented the struggle for women's rights and equality, such a view would be laughed at and roundly condemned. Yet when someone pulls all kinds of zany interpretations out of Revelation, without any regard for what the apocalyptic genre that Revelation is so much a part of actually does and means, people are impressed. Indeed, people are often nonplused and even upset when the mythical belief that the book is all about today's headlines is shattered. But apocalyptic literature was not written to contain carefully finessed doctrines of the end times. It was not written in secret code, waiting thousands of years until someone finally found the magic decoder ring necessary so that today's readers can finally understand it. It was not written to give esoteric forecasts of distant world events that no first century reader would ever see. That is simply not what apocalyptic literature does. Thus, perhaps the best advice anyone can give to a reader of Revelation is to simply be content with the straightforward (and in some ways rather obvious) truths that apocalyptic literature is all about. Trying to force Revelation to do more than apocalyptic literature does can only result in an interpretive disaster.

That means, secondly, we must keep the main thing the main thing. In apocalyptic literature the main idea is centered on two truths. First, apocalypses affirm that God is in control. Order and justice may appear to be breaking down. Right may appear to be losing to wrong. The forces of darkness may seem to have the upper hand. None of that is true. God is absolutely and firmly in control. He is sovereign and all things that happen are happening by His decree or by His permission or both. Nothing surprises Him, and nothing can overthrow His purposes. It is God who sits on the throne of the universe (4:2ff), reigning and ruling over everything and everyone (4:11). Repeatedly, Revelation shows God directing, doing, causing and controlling all that happens as His will is brought to pass without fail (note chs. 8-9; 11:17-18; 16:7; 17:1ff; 18:5, 20; 19:2, 6; 20:9-15).

The fact that today's readers of Revelation seem to overlook this obvious message may say more about our current world than we wish. Why aren't more people interested in the sovereignty of God? Could it be because so many today imagine they are in control and thus they do not need God? With wealth and power and technology there are many ways of exerting our will on our environment, surroundings, and society. We feel safe and secure in our constitutional liberties, and we know a good lawyer if someone presumed to try and breach them. We have money saved for retirement, and health insurance if we get sick. We are, it is easy to believe, in control of our world. Indeed, one of the chief complaints people often have about prayer is that it does not work, which usually means that God is not getting our will done fast enough so we can remain firmly in control of our own little kingdom.

When people are persecuted, all such illusions of control go away. Persecution means homes and businesses are confiscated. People's liberty and even lives can be taken away. Pain and suffering of the worst kind replace leisure and prosperity. Those first century saints being pounded on the anvil of persecution needed a message reassuring them that the world was not off its tracks and that they could still count on God. That is one of the primary purposes of apocalyptic literature.

It is worth noting here that the emphasis on God's sovereignty assures readers of biblical apocalyptic literature that history is going somewhere. In the horror of persecution and the confusion and chaos of such dark times, it is easy for one to think, "This Christianity stuff is all pointless." But, Revelation says it is not. All of history is pointed toward one final Day when God will sort everything out, and every wrong will be answered for and every evildoer punished. Revelation 20 and 21 show the great throne judgments and carefully details that those who give up on the Lord, who in fear and cowardice go back on their commitment to Him, will be placed "in the lake that burns with fire and sulfur" (21:8). History is moving forward, inexorably, to that judgment scene. What we witness here is only the visible earthly battles of the great war being played out in heavenly places, a battle that Revelation assures us God will surely win. Therefore, Christianity and discipleship, when set in the context of apocalyptic literature's explanation of reality, have profound meaning and purpose.

That establishes then another dominant point of apocalyptic: to encourage its readers to perseverance and faithfulness during harsh times (see Revelation 2:10; 13:10; 14:12). If God's rule and reign are firmly established, if God's purposes will be fulfilled, then only a fool would desert the Lord for a few moments of temporary security in this world. The priority of this message becomes crystal clear when once again the New Testament times are considered. What sense does it make to serve God if doing so makes one the target of vicious persecution? Suffering miserably, losing all one owns, and even being put to death for some spiritual cause does not appear to be very smart to most people. Serving God under the terms of the Deuteronomic covenant ("be faithful and I will bless you") is a no-brainer. People understand being blessed for being faithful. What about serving God when it brings a curse instead of a blessing? Only apocalyptic writings could answer such a question, and its answer was that serving God brings enormous blessing *in the life to come*, so do not be seduced by the present times. "Stand fast

for righteousness and serve the Lord" is the message not just of Revelation but also of apocalyptic literature in general. This is an enormous main theme, with tremendous practical implications for the reader. Readers of Revelation must keep this truth firmly in view at all times. Of course, what is wonderful about apocalyptic literature is that this is not difficult to do because there is not anything subtle about such writings! Still somehow this message gets buried under an avalanche of far more creative and contemporary (and speculative) approaches to Revelation. Finding an appreciation for the genre of apocalyptic literature frees us to let the main thing be the main thing.

Before proceeding further, we want to combine these first two ideas. We have learned that we must not press Revelation to do more than it wants to do. Furthermore, we have learned that it wants to establish God's sovereignty and encourage faithfulness in the midst of persecution. What does this mean? It means that if one reads Revelation and comes away from that reading deeply impressed with God's power, might, and control over all things and is encouraged to remain true and loyal to Him... *that person understood the book of Revelation.* The reader saw what the book wanted him or her to see and understand. There is not more hiding under the left sandal of a mighty angel, or obscured by the long hair of a man-eating locust. Revelation tells us that Jesus and the devil got in a fight and Jesus won. Holding on to that main idea not only means one can understand Revelation, it is the understanding Revelation wants the reader to have.

Sadly, somehow this profound but simple idea hardly seems to satisfy. It is very tempting to demand more out of Revelation. Many are sure there is something else *more* in there. Perhaps in some ways that is understandable, particularly since simplifying twenty-two chapters down to "God is sovereign, so be faithful" seems to be a trifle concise. Of course, Revelation does teach other truths (such as evil is awful or that men and women often resist the call to repent). But other themes and ideas must not be allowed to upstage the main truth of God's reign and rule and the need for everyone to submit to and faithfully obey God. The book wants its readers to get those two truths, and it pounds them home with relentless ferocity. When readers understand those truths, they have perceived Revelation's apocalyptic message, and as a result, they are rewarded with understanding the book.

This is certainly how it works in other books of the Bible. If one reads the Gospel of Luke and summarizes it by saying, "This book shows that Jesus came to seek and save the lost" (see Luke 19:10), everyone would recognize this summary represents the main focus in Luke's Gospel. The person who reads Luke's Gospel and comes away with that understanding "gets it." In the same way, therefore, this book argues that the person who reads Revelation and says, "God is in control and I must be faithful to Him," gets it. He or she understands the main message of Revelation, and indeed, even has a framework to fit in other truths that amplify and support that main message.

The reader may be further helped by a third key idea: never forget the time frame of apocalyptic literature. This is particularly helpful in guarding against wrong uses of Revelation and much of the false doctrine that has been derived from it. Fanciful interpretations that shove today's current events into Revelation cannot carry much weight with people who know apocalyptic literature and the apocalyptic genre. Reading from *1 Enoch* or the *War Scroll* makes a difference in how one views and understands Revelation from that point forward. But what does one do when presented with some outlandish view of Revelation from someone who does not know anything about the apocalyptic genre? If one answers, "Go read *The Animal Apocalypse*" he is not offering an effective response.

What may be more effective here is to point to Revelation's fixation on immediate solutions. Reading apocalyptic literature reveals that this is true in nearly all writings of this genre. Apocalyptic literature is designed to encourage faithfulness under fire, and one of the chief ways it does so is to constantly assert that God will act decisively to save His people and judge evildoers, and that this great action of God will come very, very soon. So 4 Ezra 14:10-12 says, "For the age has lost its youth, and the times begin to grow old. For the age is divided into twelve parts, and nine of its parts have already past, as well as half of the tenth." All of world history is composed of twelve parts, and Ezra is told nine and a half of those parts have already passed! "The end is near" is not just a slogan in apocalyptic literature, it is a constant refrain. In apocalyptic literature the time frame is *now*, and it is *now* that matters because its readers are placed so close to the end of all things. This kind of language is a constant in apocalyptic because telling readers God will save the faithful thousands of years from now is just not very encouraging. The operative words in apocalyptic are "soon" and "quickly." But one does not need familiarity with *2 Baruch* or *The Animal Apocalypse* to know this. Revelation itself repeatedly states that its message is for its original readers because they would see the events and deliverance the book promises. Its readers are advised how its events "must soon take place" (1:1) and the "time is near" (1:3). At the end of Revelation these ideas surface again as the coming of Jesus is stated as being "soon" three times (22:7, 12, 20).

This is a powerful defense against making mistakes with Revelation. If someone wants to argue that Revelation is about the United Nations forming a one-world government under the direction of a soon-to-be-recognized-charismatic anti-Christ, all they must explain is how such a view does not directly contradict the book's stated time frames. It might be nice to hear how this UN action was supposed to reassure and comfort first century disciples, but if that is too much to ask for, at least all can agree that Revelation claims something dramatic will happen soon. That something, in Revelation, is the relief of persecuted Christians by the destruction of their enemies. There might be considerable debate about the who and what of that fulfillment, but there can be no debate about the when. So most speculative theories injected into Revelation meet their Waterloo here. Revelation does not address life in our times because that was of no interest or help to its original audiences. Like all other apocalyptic works, Revelation is consumed with current events and immediate happenings. It promises God's actions soon. Our choices are to believe that and work with that as we read and understand Revelation, or decide that the book somehow deceived its first century readers.

Finally, what is most important about reading Revelation is that the reader must allow its truths to work in his or her life. John Collins writes "apocalyptic language is *commissive* in character: it commits us to a view of the world for the sake of the actions and attitudes that are entailed ... the apocalyptic revolution is a revolution in the imagination. It entails a challenge to view the world that is radically different from the common perception."[43] This is what sets Revelation apart from non-inspired apocalyptic writings. Non-inspired apocalyptic may teach and even help us appreciate inspired apocalyptic literature. But only Revelation is God's truth designed to change disciples to the very core. Revelation announces there is more to life than this life. Revelation says that what is seen is not all there is or all that matters. Thus, having one's eyes opened by Revelation necessarily changes how one values the world around him or her. Revelation challenges people's optimistic view of humanity and the deep belief held by most Americans that every problem can be conquered through political or technological solutions.

Reading this last book of the New Testament is a profoundly life-altering event because it forces upon the reader the apocalyptic viewpoint. That is a different way of viewing everything, and with that change in thinking must come a change in living. Is it too much to suggest that much of the misuse of Revelation comes as people conveniently sidestep the force of Revelation by projecting it to future times, military battles, and exciting foes that will arise someday? That kind of writing and preaching is fun, and interesting, and leaves people largely alone. On the other hand, people will be challenged when they understand that "Revelation says this world is evil to the core and will try to crush the followers of Christ. Will you stand up and be counted for Jesus or will you go along with the forces of darkness?" Such a challenge will never receive a kind reception. Reading Revelation correctly as apocalyptic literature makes one terribly pessimistic about this world and enormously optimistic about the world to come. Such a reading of Revelation interests very few. It means Revelation cannot be viewed at arm's length as some sort of spiritual sideshow or novelty. It is not a freak show. Revelation is a powerful way of conveying the truths that are the keys to eternal victory for its readers.

These four principles are what this book means to set forth and to offer as a way to understand Revelation's great message. We must be content with what Revelation certainly appears to be saying and not try to force it to be more. We must keep the two main truths before us. We must respect the book's emphasis on its original readers' immediate future. More than anything else, today's readers must let what Revelation says work in them to change how they see themselves, the world they are part of, and the choices they make as the battle between good and evil rages around them.

The story is told of a pickup basketball game in the gymnasium of a major seminary. Fifteen or twenty graduate students were vigorously playing basketball to work off steam from studying theology and biblical languages. During a break in the action, one of the young men noticed the custodian sitting in the stands, reading a book while he was waiting to lock up. "What are you reading there, old man?" he asked. "The book of Revelation," he replied, lifting the book slightly so that the student could see he was far into the last book of the Bible. Several of the students snickered. A custodian reading the most complex book in Scripture! A few unkind remarks were made about that, almost loud enough for the old man to hear them. One student, pushed by the swell of derision, challenged the custodian. "Do you really think you can understand what you are reading?" Without hesitation the custodian replied quietly, "Yes, I do." "Well, then, gather around boys, this is really something. Here a janitor has figured out Revelation!" sneered the student. "Come on, old man. Out with it. Give it to us. Tell us what the book of Revelation is all about." The custodian paused for only a moment. He held up his open Bible so they could all see the title page of Revelation. Pointing an aged finger directly at the page he announced emphatically, "This book means *Jesus wins!*"

A study of the apocalyptic genre, working through its definitions, goals and methodology, can lead to one and only one conclusion: the old custodian was right. It is this understanding that modern readers of Revelation need so much if they are to be blessed with renewed courage and zeal by John's apocalypse. Read Revelation. Let its incredible scenes indelibly stamp this truth deep within: Jesus wins! Then know and be assured that the message of this great book has indeed been genuinely understood.

Works Cited

Arndt, William, F. Wilbur Gingrich, Frederick W. Danker, and
    Walter Bauer, *A GreekEnglish Lexicon of the New Testament and
    Other Early Christian Literature: A Translation and Adaption of the
    Fourth Revised and Augmented Edition of Walter Bauer's
    GriechischDeutsches Worterbuch Zu Den Schrift En Des Neuen
    Testaments Und Der Ubrigen Urchristlichen Literatur.* Chicago:
    University of Chicago Press, 1996.

Baumgartner, Frederic J. *Longing for the End: A History of
    Millenialism in Western Civilization.* New York: St. Martin's
    Press, 1999.

Boring, Eugene M. "The Theology of Revelation." Interpretation 40
    1986: 260.

Caird, G.B. *A Commentary on the Revelation of St. John the Divine, 2
    volumes, International Critical Commentary.* Edinburgh: T. and T.
    Clark, 1920.

Charlesworth, James H. *The Apocalypse of Zephaniah.* October 26,
    2010.
    <http://www.christianmedia.us/apocalypseofzephaniah.html>

Collins, Adela Yarbro. *Notes on Cosmology and Eschatology in Jewish and Christian Apocalypticism*. Leiden: Brill, 2000.

Collins, John J., ed. "Apocalypse: The Morphology of a Genre." *Semeia* 14 1979: 9.

_____. *The Apocalyptic Imagination, second edition*. Grand Rapids: Eerdmans, 1998.

deSilva, David A. "The Revelation to John: A Case Study in Apocalyptic Propaganda and the Maintenance of Sectarian Identity." *Sociological Analysis* 1992, 53:4: 375.

Efird, James M. *Revelation for Today: An Apocalyptic Approach*. Nashville: Abingdon, 1989.

Frankfurter, David. "Early Christian Apocalypticism: Literature and Social World," *The Encyclopedia of Apocalypticism, ed. by Bernard McGinn, John J. Collins, and Stephen J. Stein, Volume 1*. New York: Continuum Publishing, 1998. 415.

Helyer, Larry R. *Exploring Jewish Literature of the Second Temple Period, A guide for New Testament students*. Downer's Grove, IL: IVP, 2002.

Jerome, Adam. *The Apocalypse of Abraham*. October 26, 2010. <http://www.pseudepigrapha.com/pseudepigrapha/Apocalypse_o f_Abraham.html>

Laurence, Richard. *The Book of Enoch*. October 26, 2010. <http://www.johnpratt.com/items/docs/enoch.html#14>

Lindsey, Hal Lindsey. *There's a New World Coming: "A Prophetic Odyssey."* Santa Ana, CA: Vision House, 1973.

Long, Thomas G. "Preaching Apocalyptic Literature." Review and Expositor 90 1993: 371.

MerriamWebster's *Collegiate Dictionary. Eleventh ed.* Springfield, Mass.: MerriamWebster, Inc., 2003.

Michaels, J. Ramsey. *Interpreting the Book of Revelation.* Grand Rapids: Baker, 1992.

Nickelburg, George W.E. *Ancient Judaism and Christian Origins.* Minneapolis: Fortress Press, 2003.

Thomas Nelson Publishers. T*he Holy Bible: New Revised Standard Version.* Nashville: Thomas Nelson Publishers, 1989.

Reddish, Mitchell G. ed. *Apocalyptic Literature: A Reader.* Nashville: Abingdon Press, 1990.

Russell, D. S. *Divine Disclosure: An Introduction to Jewish Apocalyptic.* Minneapolis: Fortress Press, 1992.

Stuart, Moses. *A Commentary on the Apocalypse, Volume I.* Andover: Allen, Morrill and Wardwell, New York: M.H. Newman, 1845.

Wojick, Daniel. *The End of the World as We Know It: Faith, Fatalism, and Apocalypse in America.* New York University Press: New York, 1997.

Notes

1. "Genre." *MerriamWebster's Collegiate Dictionary*. Eleventh ed. (Springfield, Mass.: MerriamWebster, Inc., 2003)
2. Frederic J. Baumgartner, *Longing for the End: A History of Millenialism in Western Civilization* (New York: St. Martin's Press, 1999) 37.
3. Baumgartner 59.
4. Baumgartner 120.
5. William Arndt, F. Wilbur Gingrich, Frederick W. Danker, and Walter Bauer, *A GreekEnglish Lexicon of the New Testament and Other Early Christian Literature: A Translation and Adaption of the Fourth Revised and Augmented Edition of Walter Bauer's GriechischDeutsches Worterbuch Zu Den Schrift En Des Neuen Testaments Und Der Ubrigen Urchristlichen Literatur* (Chicago: University of Chicago Press, 1996, c1979) 92.
6. Baumgartner 175.
7. John J. Collins, ed., "Apocalypse: The Morphology of a Genre," *Semeia* 14 (1979) 9.
8. J. Ramsey Michaels, *Interpreting the Book of Revelation* (Grand Rapids: Baker, 1992) 26.

9. The Holy Bible: *New Revised Standard Version* (Nashville: Thomas Nelson Publishers, 1989) 1 Mac 4:46.

10. The Holy Bible : *New Revised Standard Version* (Nashville: Thomas Nelson Publishers, 1989) 1 Mac 9:27.

11. Mitchell G. Reddish, ed., *Apocalyptic Literature: A Reader* (Nashville: Abingdon Press, 1990) 20.

12. D.S. Russell, *Divine Disclosure: An Introduction to Jewish Apocalyptic* (Minneapolis: Fortress Press, 1992), 14.

13. Eugene M. Boring, "The Theology of Revelation," *Interpretation* 40 (1986) 260.

14. Thomas G. Long, "Preaching Apocalyptic Literature," *Review and Expositor* 90 (1993) 371.

15. David Frankfurter writes "Through the Greco-Roman Period and especially in the latter first century C.E. with the book of Revelation, we see a widespread and pronounced interest in apocalyptic texts, otherworldly revelations in general and the whole notion of a book as medium of otherworldly gnosis. At the same time, we see widespread evidence of apocalyptic movements groups organized around an expectation of the end of the world and a conviction in their own sainthood. Many of these texts and many of these movements seem also to have embraced one or another form of Christian ideology." David Frankfurter , "Early Christian Apocalypticism: Literature and Social World," *The Encyclopedia of Apocalypticism*, ed. by Bernard McGinn, John J. Collins, and Stephen J. Stein, Volume 1 (NY: Continuum Publishing, 1998) 415.

16. Larry R. Helyer, *Exploring Jewish Literature of the Second Temple Period, A guide for New Testament students* (Downer's Grove, IL: IVP, 2002) 385.

17. George W.E. Nickelburg, *Ancient Judaism and Christian Origins*

(Minneapolis: Fortress Press, 2003) 2021.

18. Moses Stuart, *A Commentary on the Apocalypse, Volume I* (Andover: Allen, Morrill and Wardwell, New York: M.H. Newman, 1845) 126127.

19. See Michael Reddish, *Apocalyptic Literature* (Nashville: Abingdon Press, 1990) 28.

20. James M. Efird, *Revelation for Today: An Apocalyptic Approach* (Nashville: Abingdon, 1989) 24.

21. John J. Collins, *The Apocalyptic Imagination*, second edition (Grand Rapids: Eerdmans, 1998) 39.

22. Reddish 55.

23. David A. deSilva, "The Revelation to John: A Case Study in Apocalyptic Propaganda and the Maintenance of Sectarian Identity," *Sociological Analysis* (1992, 53:4) 375.

24. See Collins 250.

25. Collins 250.

26. Collins 101.

27. By 1991 *The Late Great Planet Earth* had sold more than 28 million copies. See Daniel Wojcik's, *The End of the World as We Know It: Faith, Fatalism, and Apocalypse in America* (New York University Press: New York, 1997) 37.

28. Hal Lindsey, *There's a New World Coming: "A Prophetic Odyssey"* (Santa Ana, CA: Vision House, 1973) 298.

29. Adela Yarbro Collins, *Notes on Cosmology and Eschatology in Jewish and Christian Apocalypticism* (Leiden: Brill, 2000) 68.

30. Yarbro Collins 137.

31. John J. Collins 64.

32. Adam Jerome, "The Apocalypse of Abraham," October 26, 2010, <http://www.pseudepigrapha.com/pseudepigrapha/ Apocalypse_of_Abraham.html>

33. Richard Laurence, *The Book of Enoch*, October 26, 2010, <http://www.johnpratt.com/items/docs/enoch.html#14>

34. James H. Charlesworth, *The Apocalypse of Zephaniah*, October 26, 2010, <http://www.christianmedia.us/apocalypseofzephaniah.html>

35. John J. Collins 17.

36. John J. Collins 282.

37. Reddish 35.

38. Efird 26.

39. G.B. Caird, *A Commentary on the Revelation of St. John the Divine*, 2 volumes, International Critical Commentary (Edinburgh: T. and T. Clark, 1920) 25 cited by J. Ramsey Michael 112.

40. Yarbro Collins 233.

41. Referenced by John J. Collins 168.

42. John J. Collins 17.

43. John J. Collins 283.

www.ingramcontent.com/pod-product-compliance
Lightning Source LLC
Chambersburg PA
CBHW071607040426
42452CB00008B/1266